LAURIE LEE

A Moment of War

VIKING

VIKING

Published by the Penguin Group
Penguin Books Ltd, 27 Wrights Lane, London W8 5TZ, England
Penguin Books USA Inc., 375 Hudson Street, New York, New York 10014, USA
Penguin Books Australia Ltd, Ringwood, Victoria, Australia
Penguin Books Canada Ltd, 10 Alcorn Avenue, Toronto, Ontario, Canada M4V 3B2
Penguin Books (NZ) Ltd, 182–190 Wairau Road, Auckland 10, New Zealand

Penguin Books Ltd, Registered Offices: Harmondsworth, Middlesex, England

First published 1991
5 7 9 10 8 6

Set in 12½/15½ pt Lasercomp Bembo
Printed in England by Clays Ltd, St Ives plc

A CIP catalogue record for this book is available from the British Library

ISBN 0-670-84019-X

To the defeated

Contents

1

Return and Welcome

In December 1937 I crossed the Pyrenees from France – two days on foot through the snow. I don't know why I chose December; it was just one of a number of idiocies I committed at the time. But on the second night, near the frontier, I was guided over the last peak by a shepherd and directed down a path to a small mountain farmhouse.

It was dark when I reached it – a boulder among boulders – and I knocked on the door, which was presently opened by a young man with a rifle. He held up a lantern to my face and studied me closely, and I saw that he was wearing the Republican armband.

'I've come to join you,' I said.

'*Pase usted,*' he answered.

I was back in Spain, with a winter of war before me.

The young man slung his rifle over his shoulder and motioned me to enter the hut. A dark passage led to a smoky room. Inside, in a group, stood an old man and woman, another youth with a gun, and a gaunt little girl about eleven years old. They were huddled together like a family photograph fixing me with glassy teeth-set smiles.

There was a motionless silence while they took me in – seeing a young tattered stranger, coatless and soaked to the knees, carrying a kit-bag from which a violin bow protruded. Suddenly the old woman said 'Ay!' and beckoned me to the fire, which was piled high with glowing pine cones.

I crouched, thawing out by the choking fumes, sensing deeply this moment of arrival. I felt it first when threading through the high rocks of the frontier, when, almost by pressures in the atmosphere, and the changes of sound and scent, a great door seemed to close behind me, shutting off entirely the country I'd left; and then, as the southern Pyrenees fell away at my feet, this new one opened, with a rush of raw air, admitting all the scarred differences and immensities of Spain. At my back was the tang of Gauloises and slumberous sauces, scented flesh and opulent farmlands; before me, still ghostly, was all I remembered – the whiff of rags and wood-smoke, the salt of dried fish, sour wine and sickness, stone and thorn, old horses and rotting leather.

'Will you eat?' asked the woman.

'Don't be mad,' said her husband.

He cleared part of the table, and the old woman

gave me a spoon and a plate. At the other end the little girl was cleaning a gun, frowning, tongue out, as though doing her homework. An old black cooking-pot hung over the smouldering pine cones, from which the woman ladled me out some soup. It was hot, though thin, a watery mystery that might have been the tenth boiling of the bones of a hare. As I ate, my clothes steaming, shivering and warming up, the boys knelt by the doorway, hugging their rifles and watching me. Everybody watched me except for the gun-cleaning girl who was intent on more urgent matters. But I could not, from my appearance, offer much of a threat, save for the mysterious bundle I carried. Even so, the first suspicious silence ended; a light joky whispering seemed to fill the room.

'What are you?'

'I'm English.'

'Ah, yes – he's English.'

They nodded to each other with grave politeness.

'And how did you come here perhaps?'

'I came over the mountain.'

'Yes, he walked over the mountain . . . on foot.'

They were all round me at the table now as I ate my soup, all pulling at their eyes and winking, nodding delightedly and repeating everything I said, as though humouring a child just learning to speak.

'He's come to join us,' said one of the youths;

and that set them off again, and even the girl lifted her gaunt head and simpered. But I was pleased too, pleased that I managed to get here so easily after two days' wandering among peaks and blizzards. I was here now with friends. Behind me was peace-engorged France. The people in the kitchen were a people stripped for war – the men smoking beech leaves, the soup reduced to near water; around us hand-grenades hanging on the walls like strings of onions, muskets and cartridge-belts piled in the corner, and open orange-boxes packed with silver bullets like fish. War was still so local then, it was like stepping into another room. And this was what I had come to re-visit. But I was now awash with sleep, hearing the blurred murmuring of voices and feeling the rocks of Spain under my feet. The men's eyes grew narrower, watching the unexpected stranger, and his lumpy belongings drying by the fire. Then the old woman came and took me by the elbow and led me upstairs and one of the boys followed close behind. I was shown into a small windowless room of bare white-washed stone containing a large iron bed smothered with goatskins. I lay down exhausted, and the old woman put an oil lamp on the floor, placed a cold hand on my brow, and left me with a gruff good-night. The room had no door, just an opening in the wall, and the boy stretched himself languidly across the threshold. He lay on his side, his chin resting on the stock of his gun, watching me with large black unblinking eyes. As I slipped into sleep I remembered I had left all my baggage downstairs; but it didn't seem to matter now.

I was awoken early next morning by the two armed brothers who were dressed for outdoors in ponchos of rabbit skin. They gave me a bucket of snow to wash in, then led me gingerly downstairs and sat me on a stool where the old lady poured me some coffee. The little girl, her hair brushed and shining already, was fitting ammunition into cartridge-belts. As I drank my coffee – which tasted of rusty buttons – she looked at me with radiant slyness.

'He came over the mountains,' she said perkily, nodding to herself.

The boys giggled, and the old man coughed.

They brought me my baggage and helped me sling it over my shoulders, and told me that a horse and cart were waiting for me outside.

'They sent it up from the town specially. They didn't want to keep you hanging about ... Well, not after you came all that way to join us.'

The boys half-marched me into the lane and the rest of the family followed and stood watching, blowing on their purple fingers. The old woman and child had bright shawls on their heads, while, for some reason, the old man wore a tall top hat.

The cart waiting in the lane resembled a rough-looking tumbril, and the driver had a cavernous, nervous face. 'Vamanos, vamanos, vamanos,' he kept muttering plaintively, giving me glances of sharp distaste.

The boys helped me into the back of the cart and climbed up after me.

'Here he is. The English one,' they said with ponderous jocularity.

The driver sniffed, and uncoiled his whip.

'Horse and cart,' said one of the brothers, nudging me smartly. 'We've got to save your legs. They must be half destroyed with all this walking over mountains. And what have we got if we haven't got your legs? You wouldn't be much use to us, would you?'

I was beginning to get a bit bored with all this levity, and sat there silent and shivering. The boys perched close beside me, one on each side, holding their guns at the ready, like sentries. Every so often they pointed them at me and nodded brightly. They appeared to be in a state of nervous high spirits. 'Vamanos!' snarled the driver, and shook up the reins crossly. The old man and his wife raised their hands solemnly and told me to go with God. The little girl threw a stone at the horse, or it may have been at me, but it hit the horse and caused it to start with a jerk. So we began to lumber and creak

down the steep rocky lane, the brothers now holding me by either elbow. The Pyrenees stood high
behind us, white and hard, their peaks colouring to
the rising sun. The boys nodded towards them,
grinning, nudging me sharply again, and baring
their chestnut-tinted teeth.

Through the iced winter morning, slipping over
glassy rocks, we made our stumbling way down the
valley, passing snow-covered villages, empty and
bare, from which all life and sound seemed with-
drawn. This chilling silence was surely not one of
nature, which could be broken by a goat-bell or the
chirp of a bird. It was as if a paralysing pestilence
had visited the place, and I was to notice it on a
number of occasions in the weeks to come. It was
simply the stupefying numbness of war.

After an hour or so we came to a small hill town
still shuttered by the shadow of rocks. A bent
woman crept by, bearing a great load of firewood.
A cat shot through a hole in a wall. I noticed that
the brothers had suddenly grown tense and anxious,
sitting straight as pillars, thin-lipped, beside me.
Two militiamen, in khaki ponchos, came out of a
doorway and marched ahead of us down the street.
Even our driver perked up and began to look
around him with what appeared to be an air of
importance. The militiamen led us into the square,
to the dilapidated Town Hall, from which the

Republican flag was hanging. The brothers called out to a couple of sentries who were sitting on the steps, and one of them got up and went inside. Now for a proper welcome, I thought. I got down from the cart, and the brothers followed. Then four soldiers came out with fixed bayonets.

'We've brought you the spy,' said the brothers, and pushed me forward. The soldiers closed round me and handcuffed my wrists.

They put me in a cellar and left me for two days. I got a kind of soup the first day, and they forgot me the next – waiting and forgetting being just another part of the war. It was damp and very cold, the walls of the cellar limed with ice like spidery veins of lace. But luckily I'd been toughened up by the cottage bedrooms of home where the water in wash-basins froze solid in winter. The cell had a curious, narrow, coffin-like shape, and even had iron rings round the walls as though to lift it up from inside. There was one dim, yellow-coloured light-bulb hanging from the ceiling, but no furniture; I slept on the rocky floor.

Lying there, shivering, unvisited, well on into the third day, I was wondering idly what now might happen. This was not, after all, quite what I had expected. I had walked into a country at war uninvited and unannounced, and had found no comradely welcome, only suspicion and silence. I am surprised now how little surprised I was then, but I was soon to learn how natural this was.

Captain Perez was again not what I'd expected. He came for me in the late afternoon of the third day, opening my cellar door with a light whispering key. No whiskered revolutionary he, but a slim tailored dandy, a smart gleaming figure in elegantly belted uniform, and with riding boots so glazed and polished his legs appeared to be chocolate-coated. He smiled at me from the doorway, and held out a tin mug of coffee.

'Are you rested?' he asked, in a soft furry voice.

I took the coffee and drank it, hunched up on the floor, while he fetched in two chairs and placed them facing each other.

'Please sit down,' he said gently. 'Or, rather, stand up and sit down.' And he gave a sharp little affected laugh.

The officer seemed to have sleepy eyes and a lazy manner, but once seated in front of me his attitude became abrupt and clinical. How, where and why had I come to Spain? When I told him, he shook his head sadly.

'No, señor! Not over the Pyrenees. Not with all that circus equipment you were carrying. Books, cameras – and a violin, dear Jesus.' He laid a delicate warm hand on my knee. 'You know what we think, young friend? Not over the mountains – no. You came from the sea. You were landed by boat or submarine. From Bremen, was it? You mustn't be surprised that we know all this. We even know what you've come to do.'

He smiled with cream-faced satisfaction, shaking his head against my denials and explanations, and giving my knee another squeeze.

'But, comrade,' I said.

'Captain Perez,' he corrected.

'If you don't believe me, you've got my pass-port.'

'We've got dozens, dear boy. All of them phonies. And we've got an office that turns out twenty a day.' He looked at me solemnly. 'It was the violin that did it. And the German accent. You would never fool anyone, you know.'

He rose and went to the door, and clapped his hands. There was a heavy marching of feet. The four guards I'd seen earlier came tumbling into the cellar, so wrapped up there was scarcely space for the lot of us. But they circled me close in a friendly manner, trying to keep their bayonets out of each other's eyes.

'Go with them,' said the officer. 'They'll look after you.' And he stepped back into the passage to make room. As we went past him, he snapped a salute in farewell – shining, oiled and immaculate, the last of his kind I was to see in that war.

The guards marched me out into the courtyard and it was night already, with a freezing moon in the sky. The town was empty and silent, dark and shut-tered, not even a child or dog could be heard. My guards clumped beside me, jogging me along by the elbows, relaxed now, puffing and whistling. They were all rather short, like Tartars; vapour billowed from their nostrils. The shortest one spun his rifle and grinned up in my face. 'Well,' he said. 'You come a long way to see us. Over the moun-tains? That's what we hear.' 'That's right,' I said. 'Well, we're nearly there,' he said. 'You won't have to march around much longer.'

Truly we didn't go far – down a short alley and into a rough moonlit scrapyard – till we came to a hole in the ground. The men cleared the snow round the edge, and raised a metal cover, and into the dark cavity they dropped me. It was not very deep – about six to eight feet, narrow, and walled with rock. 'Good-night, Rubio,' they called. 'Warmer down there than on the mountain tops. In this weather, you understand?' They lowered the iron cover over my head and secured it with heavy bolts. Then I heard them stamping away in the snow, and I was alone again.

The hole was wider at the bottom than at the top, and I curled up on some damp, mouldy straw. The darkness was absolute; I couldn't even see the stars through the grille. Drawing up my knees to my chin, and blowing on my fingers, I now began to consider my position. I was still not altogether surprised at what was happening to me. Indeed, I was letting it happen without question or protest. But since my arrival in Spain something quite unexpected had taken over, and I don't think I realized at that stage how sinister it might be, or what grave peril I had got myself into.

I knew I was not the only one to have wandered over the frontier to join the Republicans. There must have been other volunteers who arrived alone – but were they then always dropped into dark little holes like this? Could it be some sort of discipline to test us out, to prove our loyalty of mind?

I was cold and hungry now, and in this black icy silence I began to get a sharpening taste of danger. No, thought I, this was clearly not a normal reception. The first two shivering days in the Town Hall cell may simply have been a matter of form. But then to have been cast headlong into this medieval pit seemed to suggest that I'd been picked out for something special.

But still my situation didn't disturb me too much, but rather injected me with a sharp sting of adventure. I was at that flush of youth which never doubts self-survival, that idiot belief in luck and a uniquely charmed life, without which illusion few wars would be possible. I felt the seal of fate on me, and a certain grim intoxication, alone in this buried silence. But macabre as things were, I had no idea then how very near to death I was . . .

It may have been a couple of days, or but a few hours, later that I heard the shuffle of returning feet overhead. The iron cover was removed; I saw a brief flash of stars, and another prisoner was dropped into the hole beside me. 'Now you've got a committee!' a voice called down, and the cover was lowered and bolted and the shuffling feet went away.

We stood close together in the darkness, each other's prisoner now, and twin gaolers, in this tomb of rock. 'They sent this for you,' he said, and his hands found me blindly, and I took the hard piece of broken bread. There was just room for both of us if we lay down together; I couldn't see him but at least the air grew warmer. For about a week we shared this black cave together, visited only at night by the guards overhead, who unbolted the manhole and briefly raised it while they lowered us bread, watered wine, and a bucket.

Strange being huddled so close and for so long to another human being whose face one was unable to see. I knew him to be young by his voice and breath and the chance touch of his hand when sharing food or wine. He also had a fresh wild smell about him, an outdoor smell, a mixture of pine and olives. I remember we slept a good deal, prey to an extraordinary lassitude, and, in the intervals, we talked. He was a deserter, he said; and seemed quite cheerful about it, laughing at the looking-glass differences between us. I was trying to get into the war, and he was trying to get out of it, and here we were, stuffed into the same black hole. I'd come over the mountains from France, and he'd been caught going the other way, and most certainly now, he said, we'd both be shot.

And why not, indeed? The deserter appeared quite fatalistic about it. Patiently, drowsily, with no complaint or self-pity, my companion explained the situation to me. The Civil War was eighteen months old, and entering a bitter winter. The Republican forces were in retreat and could afford to take no chances. Franco's rebels were better armed, and had powerful allies abroad, while our side had few weapons, few friends, almost no food, and had learnt to trust no one but the dead. What could you expect them to do with a couple of doubtful characters like us? They couldn't afford to keep us, feed us, or even turn us loose. Even less could they afford the luxury of a trial. So it was thought safer, and quicker, that anyone under suspicion be shot, and this was being done regretfully as a matter of course.

My companion was called Dino, he said, and he

was twenty-two years old, and he came from a little village in the Guadarramas. When his village had been burnt by the Moors, in the early days, he'd run with his younger brother through the lines and become a dynamiter. They'd worked alone, and he'd seen his brother blown up when some of the fuses went wrong. He'd fought at Guadalajara, but didn't like that kind of warfare – mostly hanging about in ditches, then massacre and panic – so he'd taken off again and headed north for France. He'd been picked up twice, and had twice got away, but he reckoned they'd collared him now for good. He knew what to expect, yes sir. He'd seen quite a number of prisoners and deserters shot, and spoke of the Republicans' methods of execution – casual, informal, often good-humoured. Locked in the dark with Dino, and listening to him describe these scenes in his soft, joky voice, I drew steadily, as I thought, towards my hour, and wondered which of the two of us would be called out first.

When it came, it came suddenly, with us both half-asleep, the iron trap-door above raised with a swift muted action, and a low voice calling the young deserter's name, giving us just time enough for a quick fumbling handshake.

As they raised Dino towards the opening he lifted his arms, and I saw his face in a brief glimmer of moonlight. It was thin and hollow, his eyes huge

15

and glowing, his long pointed countenance like an El Greco saint ascending. Finally two dark shapes pulled him through the narrow entrance, and the manhole was lowered again. I heard the clink of glasses, some moments of casual chatter, Dino's short laugh, then a pistol shot . . .

I'd been standing propped against the wall and listening, and now that it was over I slumped back on the straw. My hand touched the deserter's forage-cap, which he'd left behind. It was damp with sweat and still warm from his head.

A few days later, in the red light of dawn, the grille was dragged open and a voice called, 'Hey, Rubio! . . .' Arms reached down to help me, hands caught my wrists, and I was lifted bodily out of the sepulchre.

My legs were shaking, but I put this down to two weeks without exercise; and the dawn light stung my eyes. Was it my turn now? The courtyard glittered with snow; and the hurried preparations which I'd expected – the chair, the hand-cart, the plain wooden box, the sleepy officer with the bottle of coñac, the ragged soldiers lined up and looking at their feet – all were present. But not for me. Another young man sat bound to the chair, smoking furiously and chattering like a parrot.

But I was guided quickly across the yard and out

into the lane, where two armed guards stood waiting beside a black battered car. They pushed me into the back seat and sat one on each side of me. A broad man in a hat sat up in front by the driver.

We drove fast and silently through the hunched unhappy town and out into the empty country. We climbed a poor bumpy road on to a desolate plateau across which the wind swept pink ruffles of snow. A plateau of scattered rock and thorn, and a few bent bushes, and the wide winter sky closing in.

It became hot and airless in the car, and the guards, in their heavy brown overcoats, began to steam like sweating horses. Their nostrils steamed too, and their noses shone, and dripped on the bayonets held between their knees.

They were an odd-looking couple, the guards – one small and clownlike, with bright blue chin, the other pink and chubby, a mother's boy. I tried to talk to them, but they wouldn't answer; though one whistled knowingly between his teeth. We drove fast, swaying together on the curves, along a road that was both empty and drear.

Where were we going, and what was in store for me? In spite of the guards' silence, I felt I knew this already. Something irrevocable had taken charge which could neither be reversed nor halted, some mad scrambling of language and understanding which had already misjudged my naïve reasons for being here. I didn't realize then how normal it was for anyone, if put through the right preliminaries, to be swamped by guilt.

Since my sudden arrest and imprisonment, which at first I'd been ready to accept as some light charade touched with military confusion, I felt myself sinking, more and more, into the hands of some obscure accusation against which I ceased to look for an answer.

As the sun rose higher and whitened the rocks, the landscape turned blank, as though over-exposed. And with the whistling guards on each side of me, and the bully-shouldered officer up front, I was sure I was on the road to my doom. As my eyes grew used to the light – after all, I'd been two weeks in darkness – I saw the landscape shudder into shape, grow even more desolate and brutal. Yet never more precious as it floated past me, the worn-out skin of this irreplaceable world, marked here and there by the scribbled signs of man, a broken thatched cabin, or a terraced slope. Every breath I took now seemed rich and stolen, in spite of the oil-fumed heat in the car. Even the two armed guards, grotesque and scruffy as they were, began to take on the power and beauty of fates, protectors or destroyers, who held one's thread of life in their hands.

We'd been driving, I guessed, for about an hour,

when the officer suddenly straightened up and snapped his fingers, and we pulled off the road and stopped. The dead icy tableland crept with yellow mist, and seemed quite empty save for a clump of trees in the distance. I was ordered out of the car, one of the guards stuck a gun in my back, pointed to the trees and said, 'March!'

Why had they brought me all this way, I wondered. They could have done the job more snugly back in the gaol. Yet the place seemed apt and fitting enough; no doubt they'd used it before. The officer was out of the car now, coughing and spitting, and he came and gave my shoulder a light little shove. 'Come on, Rubio,' he said, 'Come on, march – let's go.' So I put up my head and marched . . .

I saw the vast cold sky and the stony plain and I began to walk towards the distant trees. I heard the soldiers behind me slip the bolts on their rifles. This then, of course, could be the chosen place – the plateau ringed by rock, the late dawn on our breath, the empty silence around us, the little wood ahead, all set for quiet execution or murder. I felt the sharp edges of the stones under my thin-soled shoes. The guards behind me shuttled the bolts of their guns.

If my moment was coming – and I now felt certain it was – I told myself not to look back. My intentions were simple. If they gave me enough

19

time, and I was able to reach the little wood ahead of them, that would be my last chance – and I'd make a break for it. The nearest wind-bent tree looked a thousand years old, its roots pouring over the rocks like wax. The guards were snuffling behind me. Would I reach it before they fired? Would I hear the blast before the thumping bullets hit me? Would I hear anything before the dark? I walked slowly, almost mincingly, trying not to appear to hurry. I reached the trees and prepared to run . . .

One of the guards came up behind me and took my arm. 'OK, Rubio,' he said. 'Sit down.' His comrade was already squatting under a tree and opening a tin of sardines with his bayonet. The officer and driver joined us, yawning and scratching, and we sat down in a circle together. They gave me sardines and some bread, and passed round a bottle of coñac, and as I looked at the food in my hand, and at the raw, safe landscape around me, I was seized by a brief spasm of uncontrollable happiness.

The soldiers stretched out their legs and began talking about football. The officer brushed down his clothes and rolled me a cigarette. He waved his hand at the scenery, the old trees and the rocks, and said it was his favourite spot for a picnic. They came here, he said, about twice a week. I asked him where we were going now.

'To Figueras, of course,' he said. They were going to drop me off at the Barracks. 'We thought you'd rather ride than walk.'

But he was still responsible for me, he said, if I liked to think of it that way. But only till they'd delivered me to Brigade Headquarters, then he'd be clear of me. He looked at me oddly with his hazed, blue eyes, slightly mad, amused yet cold.

Why hadn't he explained all this before? The car, the armed guards, the remote stop in the hills. Had this been another test, or some daft Spanish trick? Was he really as harmless as he appeared to be? Would he have been equally amused if I'd made that dash through the trees? There's no doubt what would have happened if I had.

2

Figueras Castle

On a bleak naked hill above the town, Figueras Castle stood like a white acropolis – a picturesque assemblage of towers and turrets, walled in by great slabs of stone. The approach road was suitably stark and forbidding, but once I'd passed inside the huge nail-studded doors, I got an impression of almost monastic calm. Indeed the Castle, clamped down on these rocks many centuries ago as a show of force commanding Spain's northern frontiers, appeared now as something a touch over-theatrical, and rather lacking any original ferocity.

But this was the 'Barracks', the place to which I had been delivered, the collecting point for volunteers entering Spain from the north. My escort, warmer and more cheerful now after several more stops on the road for anis and coñac, seemed in a natural hurry to get rid of me, and pushed me into a glass-fronted box-office just inside the gate.

'We brought you another one!' he shouted to anyone who might be listening. 'He's English, I think – or Dutch.' With that, he threw my bags across the floor, slapped me on the back, gave me a heavy-lidded wink and left.

An official, bowed at his tiny desk, looked at me with a kind of puff-eyed indifference. Then he sniffed, asked me my name and my next of kin, and wrote down my answers in a child's exercise book. As he wrote he followed the motions of the pen with his tongue, breathing hard and sniffing rhythmically as he did so. Finally, he asked for my passport and threw it into a drawer, in which I saw a number of others of different colours.

'We'll take care of that for you,' he said. 'Would you like some prophylactics?'

Not knowing what these were, I nevertheless said yes, and he handed me a bagful which I stowed away in my pocket. Next he gave me a new hundred peseta note, a forage-cap with a tassel, and said, 'You are now in the Republican Army.' He considered me dimly for a moment, then suddenly shot to his feet, raised his fist and saluted.

'Welcome, comrade!' he cried. 'You won't be here long. As soon as we collect a convoy together we pass you away. In the meantime you have training, political education, fraternal discussion, much to do. Study victory. See a doctor. Dismiss!'

He spoke with a curious accent. It could have been Catalan or French. He kicked my bags back towards me and turned away. I picked them up and went out into the courtyard.

It was now about noon, with the sun at its low winter strength, and across the northern horizon the mountains caught it like broken glass, each peak flashing with blue and white light. Away to the south the land sank in frozen waves, while to the east lay the violet sea. After my two weeks underground the light burned my eyes, and it took some while to get used to the view, focus on its range and open distances, which were immense and exhilarating. The Castle and its courtyard seemed lifted in pure blue air and pressed close to a cold clear sky. I ceased to wonder how I had got here at last. It was simply a moment of magical arrival.

The Castle courtyard was bounded by a bare white-washed wall along the top of which stood pots of crumpled geraniums. Some thirty or forty men lounged round the base of the wall, talking and smoking or eating lumps of bread. A ragged lot, dressed in an odd medley of clothes – some in civvies (as I was), others in long capes like Berbers, or in flashy jackets like white African hunters, while some had their heads thrust through jagged holes cut from the middle of military blankets.

I sat down on the edge of a little group, and was addressed in English by a chap who called himself Danny. Danny was a bone-thin Londoner, all nose and chin, with a small bent body and red wrinkled hands. He was twenty-two, an unemployed docker from Bermondsey, undernourished and frail; when he moved, his limbs seemed to flap and flutter like wallpaper on an abandoned house.

''Ere we are then, eh?' he kept saying with a kind of sneezing giggle. Over and over again. Peering at me, then at the great mountain landscape, and clasping his bony knees with his hands. 'Said I'd never make it – the lads. The old woman too. What they call this then? I got 'ere, didn't I?'

He'd clench up his tiny hands and look round him with a trembling squint. A shaking hiss came out of his thin sad mouth. 'We're 'ere then, ain't we? . . . Eh, Doug? Eh?' He turned to a man squatting beside him. 'An' 'ere's another one, eh?' he said, pointing a finger at me. 'They're coming over in bleedin' droves.'

The Scot looked at me bleakly, as though he doubted I'd be much of a reinforcement. They'd been at the Barracks a week, they said, and both showed a mixture of bravado and bewilderment, though the Scot also seemed to have a profane contempt for most of the others around him.

'Look at this bugga'' he said, jerking a finger at Danny. ''E dunno a gun fra' a stick a' rock. If we canna' do better'n tha', Guid 'elp us.'

Danny stiffened and gave him a shrivelled look.

26

'But we're 'ere then, ennit?' he said.

It was true – and we were. Danny pointed out the others gathered in the courtyard, sitting and standing in their little groups, some playing cards, or just whistling, or staring into the distance, some fast asleep with the daylight exhaustion of waiting. Everybody was here, said Danny: Dutch, Germans and Poles. Exiles from Paris, a sprinkling of thugs on the run from Marseilles, a few Welshmen from the valleys, some Durham miners, Catalans, Canadians, Americans, Czechs, and half a dozen pale and speechless Russians.

The Welsh, in their huddles, were talking Welsh. The Durham miners were protesting about the food. The Scot, who seemed to have found some brandy from somewhere, was rising on the peak of spluttering Olympian disdain.

'We gotta anni-hi-late the lot of 'em,' he growled. 'Teach 'em political authority. Or wipe 'em all out. Thas what we gotta do.'

' 'E's so drunk,' said Danny, ' 'e don't know which side 'e's on yet – do ya, you 'eathen bastard?'

Two young men, in dark suits, were playing chess on the ground, using stones in scratched squares in the sand. They were solemn, concerned, and cast disapproving glances at Doug. They talked together formally, in the accents of clerks.

This, again, was not quite what I'd expected.

In this special army I'd imagined a shoulder-to-shoulder brotherhood, a brave camaraderie joined in one purpose, not this fragmentation of national groups scattered around the courtyard talking wanly only to each other. Indeed, they seemed to share a mutual air of unease and watchfulness, of distrust and even dislike.

I left Danny and Doug and wandered casually around, pretending I'd been here for weeks. But the pattern of that first morning was to be repeated during the whole length of my stay. The French crooks crouched in corners, shrugging and scowling; the Poles sat in princely silence sunning their beautiful cheekbones. The Czechs scribbled pamphlets and passed them to each other for correction; while the Russians seemed to come and go mysteriously as by tricks of the light. The British played cards and swore.

But we were a young and unclassifiable bunch on the whole, with mixed motives and humours, waiting to test our nerves in new fields of belief. The Castle and its courtyard was our starting-point – a square of pale sunlight surrounded by snow.

How had we all got here? Some by boat, some by illegal train-shuttles from France, but most smuggled from Perpignan by lorry. I hadn't known, in my solitary ignorance, that there was this well-organized traffic for volunteers running from

London through Paris into Spain. Which was why I'd done the daft thing and come on my own, and even chosen winter to do it. Nonetheless, I heard later that my progress had not gone altogether unnoticed. I must have been watched through France, and all the way from Perpignan. Of that I was never entirely certain, but if it was true it probably saved my life.

About one o'clock that first day somebody hit a barrel with a stick and we filed into a long shed for a meal. A couple of old women handed us tin plates and spoons, then ladled out bean soup from a vat. Bean soup hot and chunky, with an interesting admixture of tar, but to me a gluttonous reward after almost two weeks of near famine in the cave.

I remembered again the concentration of the senses, of smell and flavour, that hunger brings to appetite, and with each steaming spoonful I was also aware of the grime of the unscrubbed table, the rusting metal of the soup plate, the sharp frozen landscape outside, almost the fatness of each bean.

The meal was a holiday hour, like at a refugee camp, although there were overtones of an open prison. The men sat huddled, heads down, rapidly spooning their soup, or hobbling around looking for bread; reasonably good-humoured in their ragged, unshaven selves, but showing none of the

fire and spirit I thought they should have. It seemed
we mixed at these meals – except for the French
and the Russians, who sat down, got up, and moved
about in a taciturn, self-watchful cadre.

When we'd finished eating I joined a small group
outside, sitting cross-legged in the weak afternoon
sunlight – Doug, Danny, Ulli, a Dutchman, and
Ben Shapiro, a bouncing Brooklyn Jew. We
propped ourselves stiffly against a row of white-
painted oil-drums, and those with capes wrapped
them around themselves.

First we sat in silence, inert. There seemed to be
no discipline or programme. No one of any seeming
authority came near us.

Doug said, 'I've been here ten days, and I've still
not handled a gun.'

'I've not seen one,' said Ulli.

'Too dangerous to leave lying around for the
likes of you,' said Doug.

'I have five at home,' said Ulli. 'For ducks on the
water. If I'm knowing here they're needing, I am
bringing all of them with me.'

We sat idly a little longer, then we were called in
to a lecture given by a pink-faced Belgian in a long
black mackintosh. With a series of maps and slogans
he was proving that Franco had lost the war, when
the lecture seemed to peter out through a sudden
lack of interest.

'Tomorrow is political education,' he said. 'Now is free time to go down to the town. Class dismissed.' And he picked up his maps and left.

About six of us sauntered through the Castle gates. The sentry had propped up his rifle against the wall. We found him playing with some children in the road outside and he raised a clenched fist as we passed.

Figueras had once been a fine hill town, with ordered streets and pretty houses, and open spaces for walking in the evening. War had shrivelled and emptied it, covered it with a sort of grey hapless grime so that even the windows seemed to have no reflections. The gathering twilight also seemed to bring an unnatural silence, as if all life had gone into hiding.

Down near the station, however, were a couple of low-roofed taverns, bare and cold, with streaming wet floors. Doug and Ulli led me first into one, and then into the other, where they were clearly already well known and where the stooping old women behind the bar threw up their hands at the sight of them.

They were not the taverns I remembered – those with great sweating wine-casks and glistening bottles labelled with posturing bullfighters. Indeed, I could see no drink at all, so in the second bar I asked for some coffee, and was given a glass of hot brown silt tasting of leather and rust.

'Leave all tha',' said Doug, 'an' come along wi'
us.' We went down some steps into a dim-lit cellar
whose walls were covered with anarchist posters –
vivid stark images of fists and faces, mouths crying
defiance, shouting blasts for freedom, guns and flags
held high, banners billowing with slogans, all in
bright, hard, primary colours.

A thin old man in a corner quickly turned his
back on us as we entered, bent low, and tried to
hide something under his cloak. There was a brief
flapping and squawking from between his legs as he
furtively pushed a chicken into a sack.

'All right, Josepe,' said Ulli, poking round the
littered cellar. 'Where is it? Out with it, man.'

'Ay – ay,' wheezed the ancient. 'Again the Frenchman, by God! Why don't you go away to your
country?'

Ulli, in Spanish, and Doug, with black Scots
oaths, began to bully and tease the old man till he
folded and scrabbled across the room. Mumbling of
foreign evils and the curses of war, he searched
through some sacking and turned up a stained goatskin flask.

We sat on the floor and passed it round between
us. It was a country coñac, vitriolic and burning.

Josepe kept the struggling chicken huddled under
his cloak and watched us peevishly while we drank.
The black hairy flask smelt richly of goat and resin,

the coñac of bitter oils. But it stung, and warmed us deep inside, just right for three men sitting on a cellar floor.

'Bless this place,' Doug grunted, wiping his mouth. 'I never wanna leave it – never.'

Danny came suddenly down the steps on his little web-like feet, noiseless, nose-poking, apologetic.

'Well, 'oo'd a' believed it?' he giggled. ''Ere we are again then, eh? Got a drop left for me? No offence, a' course.'

Doug looked at him with distaste, but passed him the coñac. Danny nodded jerkily to each of us, and drank.

Only a few days in Spain, ripe for Freedom and the Cause, and here we were, squatting in the cellar of a northern tavern, bullying a crazed old man and getting drunk.

When we'd emptied a third leather flask, Josepe begged plaintively for payment, and Doug gave him a new hundred peseta note.

'No, no!' whimpered Josepe, waving it away.

'Guid Goverrment money,' said Doug, screwing it into his hand. 'Take it mon – it's a soldier's wages.'

The old man bunched up his knees and hissed and grizzled, pushing at Doug with his tiny fists.

'No, no!' he wailed. 'It is not to be borne! Car-melita! Eulalia! Come!'

A slim gliding figure, as light as a greyhound, moved softly down the cellar steps. The man reached out a shaking hand and gripped the girl by the shoulder while the chicken broke from his cloak and flew into the wall.

'Where've you been, whore?' he growled, pinching the girl viciously. 'Why did you leave me again to the Frenchmen?'

She turned her head towards us.

'Give him something,' she whispered. 'Belt, scarf, cigarettes – anything. But quickly; he's going mad.'

The girl wore the tight black dress of the villages, and had long Spanish-Indian eyes. She pushed the old man up the stairs and told him to go to bed. Doug, Ulli and Danny followed behind him, singing brokenly and urging him on.

A winter sunset glow shone through a high grille in the wall, and I was aware, behind the sharp smell of coñac, of something softer and muskier. The young girl, crouching low in the shadows, had loosened her dress and was pouring brandy over her bare bruised shoulder.

She rubbed the liquor into her flesh with long brown fingers and watched me warily as she did so. Her eyes were like slivers of painted glass, glinting in the setting sun. I heard the boys upstairs stamping and singing to the breathy music of an old accordion. But I couldn't join them. I was trapped down here, in this place, this cellar, to the smell of coñac and this sleek animal girl.

She was stroking, almost licking, her upper arms, like a cat, her neck arched, her dark head bowed. She raised her eyes again, and we just stared at each other before I sat down beside her. Without a word, she handed me the flask of coñac, turned her bare shoulder towards me, and waited. Her skin was mottled by small purple bruises that ran backwards under her dress. I poured some drops of coñac into the palm of my hand and began to rub it awkwardly over her damp hot flesh. The girl sighed and stiffened, then swayed against me, leading me into a rhythm of her own.

The frayed black dress was now loose at the edges and gave way jerkily to my clumsy fingers. The girl's eyes were fixed on mine with a kind of rapt impatience. With a slight swerve of her shoulders she offered more flesh for healing. I rubbed more coñac into the palms of my hands. Slowly, as my touch followed her, she lay back on the sacking. The boys upstairs were singing 'Home on the Range'.

Apart from the quick stopping and starting of her breath, the girl was silent. The red blanket of sunset moved over her. Her thin dancer's body was now almost bare to the waist and revealed all the wispy fineness of a Persian print. It seemed that in some perverse way she wished to show both her beauty and its blemishes. Or perhaps she didn't care. She held my hands still for a moment.

'Frenchman,' she said thickly.

'English,' I said woodenly.

She shrugged, and whispered a light bubbling profanity – not Catalan but pure Andaluz. Her finger and thumb closed on my wrist like a manacle. Her body met mine with the quick twist of a snake.

When the square of sunset had at last moved away and died, we lay panting gently, and desert dry. I took a swig from the goatskin and offered it to her. She shook her head, but lay close as though to keep me warm. A short while ago she had been a thing of panicky gasps and whimpers. Now she looked into my eyes like a mother.

'My little blond man,' she said tenderly. 'Young, so young.'

'How old are you, then?' I asked.

'Fifteen . . . sixteen – who knows?' She sat up suddenly, still only half-dressed, her delicate bruised shoulders arched proudly.

'I kill him.'

'Who?'

'The old one. The grandfather. He maltreats . . . Thank God for the war.'

The chicken, huddled fluffily against the wall in

the corner, seemed now to be asleep. The girl turned and tidied me briskly, then tidied herself, settling her clothes around her sweet small limbs. Then she lifted her long loose hair and fastened it into a shining bun. The stamping and singing upstairs had stopped.

I was astonished that this hour had been so simple yet secret, the opening and closing of velvet doors. Eulalia was not the sort of Spanish girl I'd known in the past – the noisy steel-edged virgins flirting from the safety of upstairs windows, or loud arm-in-arm with other girls in the paseo, sensual, cheeky, confident of their powers, but scared to be alone with a man.

Eulalia, with her beautiful neck and shoulders, also had a quiet dignity and grace. A wantonness, too, so sudden and unexpected, I felt it was a wantonness given against her will. Or at least, if not given willingly, it was now part of her nature, the result of imposed habit and tutoring.

As she pulled on her tattered slippers, she told me she would not stay long in Figueras. She'd come from the south, she said – she didn't know where – and had been working here as a house-drudge since she was ten. Once she would have stayed on till body and mind were used up; the sexually abused slattern of some aged employer, sleeping under the stairs between calls to his room. Not any more, she was now free to do as she wished. Spain had changed, and the new country had braver uses for girls such as she. She need stay no longer with this brutal pig of an innkeeper. She would go to Madrid and be a soldier.

It had grown dark and cold in the cellar. Suddenly she turned and embraced me, wrapping me urgently in her hot thin arms.

'Frenchman!' she whispered. 'At last I have found my brother.'

'Englishman,' I said, as she slipped away.

The next morning there was an outbreak of discipline in the Barracks. Soon after daylight, scattered committees, in groups, began to gather in the courtyard. The Commandant – who was he? – strode about in mottled riding-boots and a cape, greeting us with uneasy bonhomie.

By majority votes it was agreed we should have some exercise and drill. Somebody blew on a bugle. Men sauntered out on to the parade-ground and arranged themselves in rows. Others ran away, thinking the bugle meant retreat or an air-raid.

Those who were left then marched up and down, shouting orders at each other, forming threes and fours, running at the double, falling over, falling out, standing still, arguing, and finally parading past the Commandant from several directions, while he stood on a chair saluting.

We were an uneven lot; large and small, mostly young, hollow-cheeked, ragged, pale, the sons of depressed and uneasy Europe. But confused as we were as we marched about, there seemed to be a growing urgency in our eyes. We were fumbling to find some order of courage; and there was that moment when we almost came together in line and step, and as we swept past the Commandant once again, our clenched fists raised, we felt that bursting of the chest and tightening of the throat which made heroes and warriors of us all. Even the Czechs and Russians seemed to be briefly affected and smiled faintly at one another.

That afternoon, having declared our brotherhood of purpose, we held a mass meeting in the mess shed to study the tactics of war. Several groups sat round tables shuffling dominoes into lines of battle. A military exercise was proposed, seconded and forgotten. A Russian drew arrows in charcoal on a white-washed wall – all centred on Figueras and pointing eastward, and home.

Doug swept in and out of the shed wearing a new leather jacket and leading a small Frenchman in a Verdun helmet. I sensed an air of busy intention and high resolve around me, and for the first time since I arrived heard strength in men's voices.

''Aven't they told ye?' barked Doug, briskly halting at my table, his thick Scots overlaid with

Military Academy cadences. 'They're putting on a show this afternoon. Parade at 14.00 hours sharp. And get into some decent uniform, you soft English lemon.'

We gathered in the square, blowing in the ice-sharp wind, and were given long sticks for guns. We were going to attack a 'strong point' up the hill, an enemy machine-gun position; a frontal and flank-ing assault on bare rising ground. 'The attack will be pushed home with surprise and determination,' said the Commandant. 'It happens all the time.'

We jogged up and down, playing football with stones, changing our platoons at will. Then, after rival shouts of command, of which we obeyed the loudest, we were over the wall and up the rocky hill. We could hear the machine-guns stuttering away at the top of the rise – rusty oil-drums being beaten with sticks.

Half way up, we halted. 'Well, attack!' said someone. We stood undecided, not knowing what to do. Then a fellow ahead of us threw himself face down on the ground, and began to wriggle forward and upward on his belly. So we all did the same, and it was fun for a moment – but we very soon changed our minds. As a method of progress it was slow, uncomfortable, dirty and boring. Some of us swore; I heard a man say, 'Sod this for a lark.' So a few of us got to our feet and started walking again.

The oil-drums were still rattling away up ahead, and we were sauntering up the hill in front. Almost invisible among the rocks, his bottom high in the air, Doug was shouting, 'Get yer 'eads down, you stoopid buggers!' Away in the distance, to the left and right of us, straggling lines of other chaps wriggled up the hill. It looked almost realistic, so I dropped into position again, crawling and following another man's boots.

Near the top of the hill, with the banging of the oil-drums much closer, our leaders cried, 'Forward! Adelante! Charge!' We leapt to our feet and galloped the last few yards, shouting as horribly as we could, and cast ourselves on the men who had been beating the oil-drums, who then threw up their arms and surrendered, sniggering.

Twenty minutes' crawling and sauntering up that bare open hill, and we had captured a machine-gun post, without loss. Our shouting died; it had been a famous victory. Real guns would have done for the lot of us.

We finished the day's training with an elaborate anti-tank exercise. A man covered a pram with an oil-cloth and pushed it round and round the square, while we stood in doorways and threw bottles and bricks at it. The man pushing the pram was Danny, from London. He was cross when a bottle hit him.

★

The next day, in the evening, a child brought me a message, and as soon as I was free I slipped down to the town. This time I went alone, but not immediately to Josepe's, but first to an old wine bar up near the Plaza. The first man I saw was the giraffe-necked Frenchman from the Pyrenees who had guided me over the last peak of the mountains. He'd been taciturn, gruff; 'Don't do this for everyone,' he'd said. 'Don't think we run conducted tours.' Which was exactly what he was doing, as I could see now. Beret and leather jacket, long neck still lagged with a scarf, he stood in the centre of the bar talking to a group of hatless young men, each looking slightly bewildered and carrying little packages. Smoking with rapid puffs, eyes shifting and watchful, marshalling his charges with special care, he handed each one a French cigarette, then pushed them towards the door. His coat was new, and his shoes well polished, and clearly he had walked no mountain paths lately. Perhaps he'd brought this little group across the frontier by truck. As he left the room, he brushed against me, caught my eye for a moment and winked . . .

I went down the street in the freezing rain and found Felipe's bar closed and dark. Through a crack in the shutters I could see a glimmer of candles and some old women sitting by a black wooden box. Bunches of crape hung over the mirror behind the bar which was littered with broken bottles. I was wondering why, and from whom, the message had been sent up to the Barracks. It had certainly been laconic enough. The boy had simply sidled in and asked me if I was 'Lorenzo the Frenchman', and then muttered, 'You've got to go down to Felipe's.'

I knocked on the door and presently one of the old women let me in. She asked who I was and I told her. 'Where's Don Felipe?' I said, and she showed her gums briefly, then said, 'Bang! He's gone to the angels.' She stabbed a finger at the open box, and there he was, his face black and shining like a piece of coal. 'Bang!' said the old woman again, with a titter, then crossed herself. 'God forgive him.'

Where was Eulalia? I asked. 'She went in a camion,' she said. 'An hour ago. Away over there . . .' I could get no more from her, except that the old man had been shot and that, in her opinion, he was without shame and deserved it.

Looking into the crone's bright death-excited eyes, and smelling the hot pork-fat of the candles, I knew that this was not a wake, or even a mourning, but a celebration of something cleared from their lives. I also knew that Eulalia, my murderous little dancer, had called me to show me what she'd done, but called me too late, and had gone.

3

To Albacete and the Clearing House

Ten days after my arrival at Figueras Castle enough
volunteers had gathered to make up a convoy. By
that time we were sleeping all over the place – in
tents in the courtyard, under the mess-hall tables, or
the lucky ones in the straw-filled dungeons. Day
after day, more groups of newcomers appeared –
ill-clad, crop-haired and sunken-cheeked, they were
(as I was) part of the skimmed-milk of the middle-
Thirties. You could pick out the British by their
nervous jerking heads, native air of suspicion, and
constant stream of self-effacing jokes. These, again,
could be divided up into the ex-convicts, the
alcoholics, the wizened miners, dockers, noisy
politicos and dreamy undergraduates busy scribbling manifestos and notes to their boyfriends.

We were collected now to be taken to where the
war was, or, at least, another step nearer. But what
had brought us here, anyway? My reasons seemed
simple enough, in spite of certain confusions. But so
then were those of most of the others – failure,

poverty, debt, the law, betrayal by wives or lovers – most of the usual things that sent one to foreign wars. But in our case, I believe, we shared something else, unique to us at that time – the chance to make one grand, uncomplicated gesture of personal sacrifice and faith which might never occur again. Certainly, it was the last time this century that a generation had such an opportunity before the fog of nationalism and mass-slaughter closed in.

Few of us yet knew that we had come to a war of antique muskets and jamming machine-guns, to be led by brave but bewildered amateurs. But for the moment there were no half-truths or hesitations, we had found a new freedom, almost a new morality, and discovered a new Satan – Fascism.

Not that much of this was openly discussed among us, in spite of our long hours of idle chatter. Apart from the occasional pronunciamentos of the middle-Europeans, and the undergraduates' stumbling dialectics, I remember only one outright declaration of direct concern – scribbled in charcoal on a latrine wall:

> The Fashish Bastids murdered my buddy at Huesca.
> Don't worry, pal. I've come to get them.
> (Signed) HARRY.

The morning came for us to leave. But it wouldn't be by camiones after all. The snow was too heavy. We would go by train. After a brief, ragged parade, and when we had formed into lines of three, the Commandant suddenly appeared with my baggage. 'It's all there,' he said, strapping it on to my shoulders, 'all except the camera, that is.' He gave me a sour, tired look. 'We don't expect much from you, comrade. But don't ever forget – we'll be keeping our eye on you.'

The Castle gates were thrown open, sagging loose on their hinges, and in two broken columns we shuffled down to the station. A keen, gritty snow blew over the town, through the streets, and into our faces. We passed Josepe's whose windows were now boarded up and outside which an armed militiaman huddled. On the station platform a group of old women, young girls, and a few small boys had gathered to see us off. A sombre, Doré-like scene with which I was to become familiar – the old women in black, watching with watery eyes, speechless, like guardians of the dead; the girls holding out small shrunken oranges as their most precious offerings; the boys stiff and serious, with their clenched fists raised. The station was a heavy monochrome of black clothes and old iron, lightened here and there by clouds of wintry steam. An early Victorian train stood waiting, each carriage about the size of a stage-coach, with tiny windows and wooden seats. Every man had a hunk of grey bread and a screwed-paper of olives, and with these rations we scrambled aboard.

As we readied to leave, with clanking of buffers and couplings, and sudden jerks backward and forward, the girls ran up and handed us their little oranges, with large lustrous looks in their eyes. The small boys formed a line, shouting, 'Salud, companeros!' The old women waved and wept.

I shared a compartment with a half-dozen muffled-up soldiers who had only arrived the day before, including an ill-favoured young Catalan whose pox-pitted cheeks sprouted stubble like a grave in May. Garrulous – as we all were – he declared himself to be an anarchist, but one with a pivotal sense of nationalism, which made him boast, quite properly, that having been born in Barcelona, he was no more Spanish than the rest of us.

For this reason he'd joined the Brigade. He kept slapping his chest. 'Pau Guasch,' he said. 'International Catalan, me! International damn Chinese-Russian-Catalan-Polish. No damn father, damn mother, damn God.' He'd helped burn down three churches in Gerona, he said. He'd scattered petrol, thrown a match, and said, 'Woosh!'

In the end we told him to shut up, his spluttering English was too much for us. He seemed in no way put down. He took a potato from his pocket, crossed himself before eating it, and muttered, 'Damn Trotsky, King of the Jews.'

The train jerked and clattered at an unsteady eight

48

miles an hour, often stopping, like a tired animal, for gasping periods of rest. We moved through a grey and desolate country crossed by deserted roads and scattered with empty villages that seemed to have had their eyes put out.

It was then that I began to sense for the first time something of the gaseous squalor of a country at war, an infection so deep it seemed to rot the earth, drain it of colour, life and sound. This was not the battlefield; but acts of war had been committed here, little murders, small excesses of vengeance. The landscape was plagued, stained and mottled, and all humanity seemed to have been banished from it. The normal drive of life had come to a halt, nobody stirred, even the trees looked blighted; one saw no dogs or children, horses or girls, no smoking fires or washing on lines, no one talking in doorways or walking by the river, leaning out of windows or watching the train go by – only a lifeless smear over roof and field, like something cancelled or in a coma; and here and there, at the windswept crossroads, a few soldiers huddled in drip-ping capes. Worse than a country at war, this one was at war with itself – an ultimate, more permanent wastage.

Night came, and darkness, outside and inside the train. Only the winter stars moved. We were still smoking the last or our Gauloises Bleus, stripping them down and re-rolling them into finer and even finer spills. Our faces, lit by the dim glow of our fags, hung like hazy rose masks in the shadows. Then one by one, heads nodded, fags dropped from sagging mouths, and faces faded from sight.

It was a long broken night, the windows tight shut, our bodies drawing warmth from each other. But there were too many of us packed into this tiny old carriage, and those who chose to lie on the floor soon regretted it. Long murmuring confidences, snores, sudden whimpers of nightmare, a girl's name muttered again and again, Pau Guasch howling blasphemies when a boot trod on his face, oaths in three languages when someone opened a window.

It may have been twenty hours later – waking and sleeping, arguing, telling stories, nibbling bread and olives, or just sitting in silence and gazing dully at each other – that the train slowed down to less than a walking pace and finally halted in a gasp of exhausted steam under the cheese-green lights of Valencia station.

We were to change trains here, and were promised hot food. The time was about midnight, and the great city around us showed no light as though trying to deny its existence, its miles of dark buildings giving off an air of prostration, pressed tight to the ground like turtles.

We had pulled up in a siding. A late moon was

rising. Some women arrived with buckets of stew. They moved in a quick, jerky silence, not even talking to each other, ladling out the thin broth in little frightened jabs. Suddenly one of them stopped, lifted her head, gave a panicky yelp like a puppy, dropped her food bucket and scampered away. She had heard something we had not, her ears better tuned already to the signals of what was to come.

Following her cry and departure, the others fled too. Then the station lights were switched off. An inert kind of stillness smothered the city, a stretched and expectant waiting. Then from the blank eastern sky, far out over the sea, came a fine point of sound, growing to a deep throbbing roar, advancing steadily overhead towards us. Such a sound that the women on the platform had learned to beware of, but which to us was only an aircraft at night. And which, as we listened, changed from the familiar, casual passage of peace to one of malignant purpose. The fatal sound which Spain was the first country in Europe to know, but with which most of the world would soon be visited.

Franco's airfields in Majorca, armed by Italian and German warplanes, were only a few minutes' flight from the mainland. Barcelona and Valencia lay as open cities, their defences but a few noisy and ineffectual guns.

As the bombers closed in, spreading their steady

roar above us, I felt a quick surge of unnatural excitement. I left the train, and the roofed platform, and wandered off alone to the marshalling yards some distance away. This was my first air-raid, and I wanted to meet it by myself, to taste the full brunt of it without fuss or panic. We'd already seen posters and photographs of what bombs could do to a city, slicing down through apartment blocks, leaving all their intimacies exposed – the wedding portrait on the wall, the cheap little crucifix, the broken bed hanging bare to the street – the feeling of whole families huddled together in their private caves being suddenly blasted to death in one breath. New images of outrage which Spain was the first to show us, and which in some idiot way I was impatient to share.

The bombers seemed now overhead, moving slowly, heavily, ploughing deep furrows of sound. A single searchlight switched on, then off again quickly, as though trying to cancel itself out. Then the whole silent city woke to an almost hysterical clamour, guns crackling and chattering in all directions, while long arcs of tracer-bullets looped across the sky in a brilliant skein of stars. This frantic outburst of fire lasted only a minute or two, then petered out, its panic exhausted.

The airplanes swung casually over the city, left now to their own intentions. Just a couple of dozen young men, in their rocking dim-lit cabins, and the million below them waiting their chance in the dark. A plane accelerated and went into a dive, followed by the others in a roaring procession. They swooped low and fast, guided perhaps by the late moon on the water, on the rooftops and railway tracks. Then the bombs were released – not from any great height, for the tearing shriek of their fall was short. There followed a series of thumping explosions and blasts of light as parcels of flame straddled the edge of the station. I felt the ground jump at my feet and smelt the reek of burnt dust. A bomb hit the track near the loading sheds, and two trucks sailed sideways against a halo of fire, while torn lines circled around them like ribbons. Further off an old house lit from inside like a turnip lamp, then crumpled and disappeared. A warehouse slowly expanded in the gory bloom of a direct hit, and several other fires were rooted in the distance. But it was over quickly – a little more of the city destroyed, more people burnt or buried, then the bombers turned back out to sea.

I found I'd stood out in the open and watched this air-raid on Valencia with curiosity but otherwise no emotion. I was surprised at my detachment and lack of fear. I may even have felt some queer satisfaction. It was something I learned about myself that night which I have never quite understood.

Once the planes had gone, there was little to be heard but the crackling of flames and the distant bells of a fire-engine. I was joined by two of my companions from the train, both silent, both fresh to this, as I was. A railwayman crossed the lines, groping about, bent double. We asked him if he was all right, and he said yes, but he needed help. He shone a torch on his left hand, which was smashed and bleeding, then jerked his head in the direction of the nearby street. We ran round the edge of the burning warehouse and found two little houses, also well alight. They were small working-class shops, blazing tents of tiles and beams from beneath which came an old man's cry.

'My uncle,' said the railwayman, tearing away at the smoking rubble with his one undamaged hand. 'I told him to sleep in the cinema.' The roofs collapsed suddenly, sending a skirt of sparks riffling across the road. The old man's cries ceased, and we staggered back while great curling flames took over. 'The fault is his,' said the railwayman. 'He would have been safe in the cine. He used to go there every afternoon.' He stood doubled up, staring furiously at the blazing ruin, his clothes smoking, his hands hanging black and helpless.

Walking back towards the station, we stumbled over a figure on the pavement, lying powdered white, like a dying crusader. His face and body were covered in plaster dust, and he shook violently from head to toe. We rolled him on to a couple of boards and carried him to the main platform, where several other bodies were already spread out in rows. A moaning woman held a broken child in her arms; two others lay clasped together in silence, while a bearded doctor, in a dingy white coat, just wandered up and down the platform blaspheming.

It was a small, brief horror imposed on the sleeping citizens of Valencia, and one so slight and routine, compared with what was happening elsewhere in Spain, as to be scarcely worth recording. Those few minutes' bombing I'd witnessed were simply an early essay in a new kind of warfare, soon to be known – and accepted – throughout the world.

Few acknowledged at the time that it was General Franco, the Supreme Patriot and Defender of the Christian Faith, who allowed these first trial-runs to be inflicted on the bodies of his countrymen, and who delivered up vast areas of Spain to be the living testing-grounds for Hitler's new bomber-squadrons, culminating in the annihilation of the ancient city of Guernica.

About four in the morning, with fires still burning in the distance, we were rounded up by our 'transport officer', who was rather drunk and wearing a Mongolian jacket. Round his neck, somewhat oddly, he'd slung binoculars and a tape-measure, and he scurried about, shooing us back to the train, as though our departure was part of some major logistic.

Some of the men had loud, over-excited voices, shining eyes, and brave tales of survival. Some were quiet and staring, others appeared to have slept unaware through everything.

Our new train was drawn up in another part of the station, where we found Pau Guasch carrying a basket of bread. Once crammed into our compartment he handed chunks of it round, saying we were not fit to eat such victuals. He was half-right there; the bread must have been several weeks old, and was coated with soot and plaster. He looked smug and benign as we tried to gnaw away at his bounty; in the end we swallowed it down.

The night was long and cramped as the train lumbered inland, slowly circling and climbing the escarpment of Chiclana to reach the freezing tableland of Mancha. I had known part of this plateau in the heat of high summer when it seemed to blaze and buckle like a copper sheet. Now it was as dead as the Russian steppes, an immensity of ashen snow reflecting the hard light of the winter moon. No gold path of glory, this, for youth to go to war, but a grey path of intense disquiet.

Apart from Pau Guasch, all the men in my compartment were volunteers from outside – British, Canadian, Dutch. And poor Guasch, the only true native son of the Peninsula, found himself squashed between his own natural assumption of leadership and our teasing contempt for him – the 'foreigner'. So we used him as the butt of our mindless exhaustion, pushed him around, tripped him up, trod him under our feet, and stuffed his shirt with crumbs and crusts of bread.

Fear, exasperation and cruelty gripped us, and we continued to taunt the furious little Catalan till we tired, at last, of our mirthless game and slumped one by one to sleep. We slept stiffly, uneasily, propping each other bolt upright, or toppling sideways like bottles in a basket. We were not warriors any more, but lumps of merchandise being carried to a dumping-ground.

In a bitter dawn we approached Albacete on the plain, clanking through tiny stations where groups of snow-swept women watched us dumbly as we passed them by. A lad at a level crossing, with a thin head-down horse, lifted a clenched fist for a moment, then dejectedly dropped it again. Silent old men and barefooted children, like Irish peasants of the Great Hunger, lined the sides of the tracks without gesture or greeting. We were received, as we trundled towards our military camp, not as heroic deliverers, or reinforcements for victory, but rather as another train-load of faceless prisoners seen through a squint-eyed blankness of spirit.

But as we steamed at last into Albacete station, we found that someone, at least, had dredged up some sense of occasion. We fell stiffly from the train and lined up raggedly on the platform, and were faced by a small brass band like a firing-squad. In the dead morning light they pointed their instruments at our heads and blew out a succession of tubercular blasts. Then a squat mackintoshed Commander climbed on to a box and addressed us in rasping tones. Until that moment, perhaps, cold and hungry though we were, we may still have retained some small remnants of courage. The Commander took them away from us, one by one, and left us with nothing but numb dismay.

He welcomed us briefly, mentioned our next of kin (which we were doing our best to forget), said we were the flower of Europe, thanked us for presenting our lives, reminded us of the blood and sacrifice we were about to bestow on the Cause, and drew our attention to the sinister might and awesome power of International Fascism now arrayed against us. Many valiant young comrades had preceded us, he said, had willingly laid down their lives in the Struggle, and now rested in the honoured graves of heroes in the battlefields of Guadalajara, Jarama and Brunete. He knew we would be proud to follow them, he said – then shook himself like a dog, scowled up at the sky, saluted, and turned and left us. We shuffled our feet in the slush and looked at each other; we were an unwashed and tattered lot. We were young and had expected a welcome of girls and kisses, even the prospect of bloodless glory; not till the Commander had pointed it out to us, I believe, had we seriously considered that we might die.

Our group leader came striding along the platform leading a squealing Pau Guasch by the ear. He wanted to go home, he cried; he'd got arthritis and the gripe. The group leader kicked him back into line. We formed up in threes and, led by the coughing and consumptive band, marched with sad ceremony through the streets of the town. We saw dark walls, a few posters, wet flags, sodden snow. Sleet blew from a heavy sky. I had known Spain in the bright, healing light of the sun, when even its poverty seemed coloured with pride. Albacete, this morning, was like a whipped northern slum. The women, as we passed, covered their faces with shawls.

4

Death Cell: Albacete

Albacete was all wind and knives, surrounded by the white pine-scarred immensities of La Mancha. As we marched to the barracks, other military figures on the pavements, of all shapes and adornment, greeted us with only a few hoots of derision.

At the barrack gates, our little brass band deserted us, and went trundling off down the street shaking out their crumpled instruments. Our brief moment of honour and welcome it seemed was ended; another trainload of scruffs had been duly delivered. We were formed up on the parade-ground, our soaking bags on our backs, snowflakes settling upon our beards. Two officers walked out and looked us over; a clerk with a clip-board stood by taking notes. Nothing was said to us; we were viewed as remote curiosities, while the mounting snow swirled and cut around us. Anonymous, unacknowledged, we stood shuffling and muttering; after all we had not yet been fed. But still they held us there in a kind of suspended detachment while the clerk counted and re-counted our numbers.

There was tension, and suddenly I felt specially separate from the others. Even before it happened, I knew it would happen. A soldier hurried from the main building and handed a note to one of the officers, who read it and called out my name. I raised my hand, my companions were dismissed, and I was once more taken away under guard.

Had I been marked down from the very beginning, I wondered? If so, why had I got this far? I was led away to a small room deep in one of the basements which was a jumble of filing cabinets, maps and papers. A young fair-haired officer sat at a littered desk, and he rose to his feet when I entered. He was smartly dressed, deferential, American and charming. He introduced himself as Sam.

'I'm sorry,' he said, and gave me a chair. 'I guess you've been through all this before – but something fresh has turned up . . .'

He produced my passport, which had been taken from me at Figueras, and slowly riffled through the pages. Two of them had been marked with paperclips, and he spread the book open and showed it to me. On his face was an expression of amused resignation – an unspoken 'how could you have been such a fool?'

In the spring of 1936 I'd spent a few days in Spanish Morocco, which General Franco was using as the base for his rebellion at that time, and from where, in July, he started the Civil War. But of course I didn't know this till he started flying his Moors across the Straits from there. I'd been in the very nest of intrigue, but knew nothing about it.

Sam fingered the pages of my passport with almost strained disbelief, then held it up to my eyes: Ceuta, Tetuan, Entrada, Salida – he pointed out the fatal names and dates.

'Just what were you doing there at that time – for Gawd's sake?' he asked. 'That's all we're wanting to know.'

Sam had now been joined by two short, square little Russians, both slightly bald and wearing civilian suits. Plumping themselves down, one on each side of the American, they waited in silence for me to speak.

I could now see the trouble I was in – first suspected as a spy, and now as a Fascist agent. No doubt about it either, Sam had the proof in his hand. I felt that sudden thump in the heart which I remember as a child when I'd been accused of some major though innocent blunder.

Yes, I said, in early 1936 I'd been working in a hotel near Malaga, and I'd made a quick trip to Morocco with a French student from Arles. Yes, it had been spring, but we hadn't seen much of the country, we'd spent most of our time in the rooms of small hotels, behind shutters, smoking hash. Sam sighed and passed his hand over his brow. He told me to empty my pockets.

Everything I had was laid out on the desk and the two square little men went to work. Cigarettes stripped, paper held to the light, fountain-pen unscrewed, then probed and smashed. Matches shaken out on to a blotter, then each one split down the middle. The matchbox itself also cut into sections and each piece pressed against a special lamp, as were the odd papers and my notebook and pocketbook, including a few pesetas and family photographs.

While the two squat civilians were at their meticulous inspections, searching for who knows what? – secret messages, war maps, codes, plans – Sam was reading through the papers they had discarded, and keeping up a quiet, continuous stream of questions. What was the name of the student? And where was he now? What hotels had we stayed in? And how much was I paid, and who paid me, huh? Well, it was only a short trip, I said, and the boy paid for most of it. He was the son of a rich businessman from Marseilles. Sam knew I was lying, but he didn't know why I was lying. My journey to Morocco had been solitary, innocent, but damning.

I was told to undress to my pants, and my clothes were searched carefully, including the linings and soles of my boots. Then something desperately unwished-for happened, but now too late to avoid; Sam found a packet of letters in my trouser hip-pocket. They were letters from the English girl who had followed me to the edge of France and tried to dissuade me from crossing the frontier – letters recalling the wildly passionate celebration of our last week together, a rapturous, explicit and tormenting farewell. I knew every word by heart, which were not for any other eyes. But now this neat young Bostonian, who might not have read such letters before, was scanning them earnestly line by line. He read them quite slowly, and looked up once or twice, as I stared blindly at the opposite wall. Sitting on the chair before him, I felt in every way naked, and no man before him had entered my private world. When he'd finished reading, he passed the letters back to me in silence. His face, though flushed, was as blank as mine.

Sam never referred to the letters again, but he was clearly an intense young professional, with a job to do; yet as he began to question me further – about dates, movements, intentions, motives – I was also aware of a look of dazed perplexity in his eyes, as that of a doctor who, while inquiring into one major disease, had unexpectedly stumbled on to another one altogether.

Sam's two gnome-like assistants, having taken their turn with my clothes and boots, now came and sat down, one on each side of me. They picked things up off the desk, and put them down, shook my violin and twanged the strings, and held a little photograph of my mother up to a mirror. They muttered together, asked each other questions, nodded, then just stared at me balefully. I had a feeling they wanted to take me out and hang me up by the heels, that the use of a thumbscrew might not altogether have wasted their day. Sam, on the other hand – warm-voiced, apologetic – addressed me with concerned good-nature.

'Well, I shall have to make a report,' he said. 'And it's not going to be easy. How did you manage to get into such a mess, anyway? You may seem harmless enough, but we can't take chances. You know that, for God's sake, don't you?'

'What's that mean, anyway?'

'I don't have to tell you, do I? I can't help it – none of us can. I'm sorry, but just look at yourself.'

So once again I was taken away under guard and put in a small underground room and left to my own confusions. But Sam didn't neglect me; he made sure I was warm, and brought me blankets, brandy and coffee. He sent an old woman to tidy the place and sweep and delouse it. He even sent in a girl – short and dumpy, with a tousled new look of political liberation, but she huffed and puffed and giggled so much I couldn't see across the cell for vapour.

The old woman, however, was comfort and entertainment. Doña Tomasina, from Cuenca, was a widow of fifty, whose husband, a leper, had been crushed by a rockfall in the cave where they lived. At the start of the Civil War she was starving and walked to Albacete, where she now scrubbed the barracks for two meals a day.

Tomasina was sad about me and kept pulling my shoulders back with her thumbs and doing her best to keep my spirits up. But it wasn't that easy. I'd been in this kind of trouble before and felt I'd been lucky to get out of the last lot. This time the situation was simpler, starker; my interrogators better trained, more implacable.

'But they just young men, like yourself,' said Tomasina. 'They know you don't do bad things. They play a little game with you. You laugh. That's all.'

Not they, I thought. Especially Sam's two Russians with their blue bullet-like faces. And with them around, Sam wouldn't dare.

I wondered how many times Tomasina had gone through all this – teasing and mothering other frightened young lads as they waited their blind and blundering dispatch. Her vivid dark eyes were like split sea-urchins, their jellied pupils flecked with red.

'Your papers upside down. They sort them out tomorrow. Then you walk out and back to your friends.'

But tomorrow came Sam, his cropped head shining and clean, but with a look of embarrassed exasperation on his face.

He held up my old sweat-soaked passport and stabbed his finger at the pages. 'It's these damned Moroccan stamps,' he growled. 'Spring '36. Melilla. Ceuta. Tetuan. That's where it was all cooked up, wasn't it? And what were you doing there at that time? That's what we want to know. Getting special training or something?' He slapped the passport again. 'It's all down here, you know. We can't get round it. Anywhere else, I might have got you clear.'

He'd brought me some writing paper, a pen and a folding table.

'If you want to write some letters, I'll see they get 'em,' he said. He looked at me helplessly. 'Er . . . if there's anything else you need?'

'Tomasina's getting me a new shirt.'

'New shirt? That's fine.' He was standing awkwardly by the door. 'Well . . . er . . . I guess you don't want me to explain any more?'

'No,' I said.

'Well, if we don't hear from Madrid, that's it, then,' he said.

He hung on for a moment, then raised his doubled fist. 'Jesus Christ,' he growled, and left.

I wrote a few letters that day, but they were brief. I couldn't say I was about to be shot as a spy, a saboteur, a Fascist infiltrator, a capitalist lackey – all of which had been mentioned among my accusers' more polite suggestions. I didn't have to explain the nature of my going at all. Sam and his colleagues, it seemed, had certainly gathered enough evidence against me; but as some small doubts still persisted, Sam promised that there would be no official record of my death.

So my letters were brief. Not even to my Mother did I wish to say farewell. Still less to the girl for whom my heart hungered. To either would have been to admit a clumsy folly, muddled, without point or glory. I had come to support a cause, to give my life to it, I supposed; but not to be rubbed out in a back-yard for having carried a violin over a mountain or for going to Morocco at the wrong time of the year. I sat in my tiny cell, wearing Tomasina's bright new shirt, staring at the table, the walls, and wondering how this could have happened, alternately convinced that I could take anything that came, only to be visited by recurrent moments of piercing terror.

The guards let in Tomasina at midnight, with

more brandy and a couple of candles. She was in bustling, chirrupy, rather over-heated spirits. 'You'll not stay here long,' she said brightly, skipping round me to straighten my shoulders. Anxiety, and pity, infected her smile as she lit a new candle from the stub of the old one. 'You've got to keep warm,' she said, dumping the brandy on the table. A bottle of the best, not corriente from a barrel. But it was not only brandy she'd brought me. Standing in the shadows behind her was a boy, about thirteen years old, with the dark curls and eyes of a Moor.

'Warm him,' said Tomasina, pushing the boy towards me, and as she left she touched my hand lightly. 'Lorenzo, may you go with God.'

The boy led me to the bunk and lay down shivering beside me. He seemed to be far colder than I was – or perhaps the reason was something else. 'Hurt me if you want to,' he said, and waited, his hands fluttering about my knees. Was this Sam's or Tomasina's idea? I wondered. Surely, they'd done enough? First the huffing and puffing liberated girl; then this thin little shuddering boy. Well, I could neither accept nor reject him now; God knows I was glad of any comfort that night.

Close to, I could see the long lines of disease running down his beautiful face, and a precocious hardness in his sleepy eyes. He reached me brandy and helped me to drink it; he was cold, but did his wriggling best to warm me. He kept crying my name, and sobbing farewell, and weeping theatrically as the night wore on. I had a feeling he was collecting relationships with the last moments of the condemned. He certainly seemed cheerful enough when he left in the morning. He asked me for my wrist-watch and I gave it to him.

The morning was a muddled embarrassment, without the dramatic clean sweep I'd expected and made myself ready for. Anything that followed now was bound to be fumbled, hurried and probably abominable. Things started at midday. Sam brought me a couple of cigars and a letter addressed to me care of the Socorro Rojo.

'I wasn't sure whether you'd want to have this,' he said, handling me a bulging envelope, already slashed open, and visibly crammed with sheaves of the girl's voluptuous handwriting. 'Then I thought, hell, why not? – shows she's thinking of you, anyway. Sent you five English pounds, too. Rather a pity about that . . .'

On his smooth face was that expression of guilty exasperation again. But he wasn't looking at me.

'I'll take your letters,' he said, and stuffed them in his pocket. He didn't say goodbye.

That afternoon a doctor visited me and gave me an injection and a couple of pills. Tomasina padded in and out, saying nothing, but giving me shy false smiles as though flicking my face with a handkerchief. I sat at the table drowsing through my girl's extravagant letters and inhaling their heady unforgivable magic.

About four o'clock I was handcuffed and taken under guard to a room where several militiamen were playing dominoes. They got up when I entered, and went away whistling. Through the door they left open I could see a small courtyard, and snow falling from a sunset sky.

One of the guards gave me a cigarette, the other touched my arm. 'Don't worry,' he said. 'It's easy, brother.' Patches of sweat showed through his light blue shirt. Then I heard a murmuring of voices in the next room, subdued salutations and greetings; a sliding panel in the wall was suddenly pushed back. Faces peered at me briskly, one by one – the two Russians, each with a brief nod of the head, an unknown officer in a fur-collared coat, then, framed like some fake Van Gogh freakishly elongated, appeared the unmistakable face of the giraffe-necked Frenchman who had guided me the last few steps across the mountain frontier. One look at me and he covered his eyes in mock horror.

'Oh, no!' he groaned, 'not him again, please. Turn him loose – for the love of heaven.'

He seemed to find the sight of me – manacled and doomed in Albacete's death row – more

71

diverting than anything else. He turned and spoke rapidly to his companions in the other room, and I heard his high-pitched Gallic cackle. A few orders were given, my handcuffs unlocked, and I was told to get back to the barracks. The two Russians, Tomasina, the girl, the boy, the long shivering night and day of preparation were over. Suddenly, inexplicably free again, I realized that a word from the little French guide showed him to have more power than anyone else around.

Crossing the square in the red twilight, on my way to the barracks, I met Sam striding in the opposite direction. Without a word of greeting or even a glance of recognition, he thrust into my hand the packet of farewell letters I'd written.

Restored to the ranks and the semi-liberty of a lax routine, I began meeting with veterans and took on some of their swagger. Albacete, the base camp of the 15th Brigade, was also a rest camp and clearing centre. I had arrived in Spain in a state of blank ignorance, but soon learned the realities of the times. After the atrocious battles of the late summer, particularly on the Aragon front, there was now a slight lull in the fighting. The Republican Army was left holding about a third of the country, backed by the entire east coast running from the Pyrenees to Almeria. Facing Franco, the line was a loose

bellying north–south zig-zag containing a vulnerable bulge driven by the General's forces. It was
true we had a weak salient reaching towards Por-
tugal in the west, but sweeping in a great curve to
the north-east Franco held Teruel in the mountains,
only fifty miles from the sea, and threatened to cut
the Republican territory in half.

Perilous as the situation may have been, it was a
time of crazy optimism, too, and all the talk was of
an offensive already mounted to recapture Teruel.
Troops were even now moving up the freezing
heights to surround the city. It would be an Olympian battle to turn the war.

So far it was an affair of Spanish troops only,
some suggesting our leaders wished them to be first
with the glory. So the International Brigades
'rested', in and around Albacete – patching their
battered weapons, reshuffling their battalions, feeling pretty certain they would be called on soon.

Meanwhile we newcomers and the veterans
massed in the town's damp cafés, drinking acorn
coffee and rolling cigarettes made from dried oak
leaves and mountain herbs. Paying for our drinks
with special printed money, little cards stamped
with the arms of the city. And eating beech nuts
roasted on griddles. For a military base camp there
was little formal discipline, though to keep warm
we sometimes drilled or paraded through the streets,

taking the salute of our Commanders, who stood on upturned wine barrels in the driving sleet, looking exhausted, faintly amused, or bored.

I remember the names and style of some of them still – Jock Cunningham, Pat Ryan, Tom Wintringham, Paddy O'Daire – black-bereted, black-mackintoshed, tight-belted figures; they were the obscure foreshadowers of coming events, the unofficial outriders of imminent World War, and had already learned more of what its wasting realities would be than any fuzz-brained Field Marshal in the armies of Britain or France.

Fred Copeman was another of this breed – veteran of Brunete, and once my strike leader when I was a builder's labourer in Putney. Here in Spain I saw again that hard, hungry face, even more shrunken now by battle and fatigue than by his struggles back home in the early Thirties. When he recognized me his hard eyes glittered with frosty warmth for a moment. 'The poet from the buildings,' he said. 'Never thought you'd make it.' Stoker Copeman was well known for his part in the naval mutiny of Invergordon, Scapa Flow; a rough-cut, hollow-cheeked, working-class revolutionary, and archetype of all the Commanders of the British Battalion, he was to survive the worst slaughter of the war, which was to bury so many like him, and was later to become, after his return to England,

Chief Adviser, Civil Defence, to the Metropolitan Borough of Westminster.

Beneath the speculative, often cynical, regard of such as these, we volunteers, our morale mysteriously rising, marched round Albacete shouting new-learned slogans in pigeon Spanish: 'Oo-achay-pay! No pasaran! Muera las Fascistas! Salud!'

Bullets were in our mouths if not in our rifles. Indeed, few of us had guns at all. We marched to make a noise, to keep warm, to know that we were still alive, our right arms raised high, punching the freezing air, our clenched fists closing on nothing.

I'd been received back into the barracks with some suspicion at first, and I can't say I was that surprised. You didn't get picked off the parade-ground, marched under guard to the 'dispatch house', interrogated for three days, given Tomasina's 'last rites', only to be suddenly turned free, with all your equipment intact – books, diary, violin – without questions or explanations. It was thought, quite naturally, that I'd been planted among them, and was therefore someone to be avoided.

As Danny, my weedy Cockney friend from Figueras, was quick to point out: 'We all bin worryin' abaht you, son. Still are, if you get me.' He pulled his nose with a sleazy giggle. 'When 'telligence blokes get 'old of summick, they don't normly let go of it. We reckon you bin lucky, or sumpen, aincha?'

'Just a small mistake,' I muttered, and Danny nodded: 'That's what I said, then, din' I?' For several days I was watched closely, or treated with loud, false camaraderie. Then the news got round that 'M. Giraffe', whom they all knew, had vouched for me; also that a mysterious high voice of authority in Madrid had sent a favourable word. I understood the one, but not the other. But this seemed good enough for most of them, anyway.

It was cold. We played cards. Meals were of semi-liquid corned beef, or sometimes something worse, with black frozen potatoes and beans. It was an idle time, still a time of waiting: there were arguments, flare-ups, sudden lunging fights, and dreamy liaisons in barrack-room corners. Brooklyn Ben held political classes, which were often crowded, and which painted a world free from betrayal and butchery. Speaking in his quiet, cracked voice, with its soft Jewish accent, he plumped up the dry demands of Communist dialectic into a nourishing picnic of idealism and love.

Sitting cross-legged on his bed, his forage-cap crammed on his ears, his large eyes melting with warm, brown-sugary sweetness, his message could have been a perversion in the middle of a war, but one which both veterans and newcomers – those who had seen death or sniffed the nearness of it – felt somehow the need to hear. Strangely enough, he was the only one I met who had a good word for the Fascists, calling them 'ice-cream-lolly boys' or 'kindergarten cut-throats'. His classes, advertised on the notice-board and presumably official, were crowded by old lags and new arrivals alike. After about a week, he disappeared. I heard he'd been clubbed in a side-street and carried away. 'Pro-Fascist nark,' said someone.

Many of us were now sleeping on the barrack floor, using muddy pallets of straw as mattresses. It was so cold, we were burning the army beds – breaking them at first accidentally. We fed the wood into a punched oil-drum and sat round it at night, ponchos over our shoulders. There was Doug and Danny, Guasch when we could stand him, a skeletal Swede, and a Yank with crutches – one of those legendary few who could charge a cigarette paper with tobacco, roll it, lick it, seal it and light it, and all with a single flick of one hand.

The Yank and the Swede, sculpted by flames from the fire, were scarred by something we could not know. The eyeballs of each seemed to sit easily in the face, but were almost detached, ringed by deep, luminous hollows. There was a look of exhausted madness in the features of both, backed by a languid bitterness of speech.

They were both veterans of the Aragon offensive. The Yank said he hoped the British were sending out less rubbish. The Swede said he didn't care what they sent so long as he could now go home. While saying this, he rocked gently to and fro, as though riding in a bus on a country road.

'You won't get home,' said the Yank. 'You still got your legs – the Army can use you yet.'

He quickly rolled him a cigarette and held it to his mouth. The Swede licked it, then sucked and gasped.

The Aragon was a cock-up, the Yank said. No artillery, no planes, no timing, no leaders, everybody running around like rabbits. He was a machine-gunner, had a beautiful Dichterer, too – only they gave him the wrong ammunition. That's why he had his ass shot off. Lucky to be alive. None of his pals were left.

They were guarding a hill near Belchite, when the Fascists counter-attacked. They were surrounded; couldn't shoot or run. Some Moors took his pals prisoner, and cut their throats, one by one; then they dropped him off a bridge and broke his legs. He lay for two days, semi-conscious, then dragged himself to the road. The front had shifted, and he was picked up by a battalion bread-van.

He told the story in gritty, throwaway lines – quietly savage, but with no dramatics. 'We were set up, goddam it. Lambs for the slaughter. No pasaran! They pasaranned all over us.' He described with light affectation the Spanish officer who had supervised the throat-cutting, the blood on his shirt and his pansy white hands.

'And d'you know what they gave me when I got back?' he said. 'A kind of welcome home, I guess.' He slowly shifted his crutches, unhooked something from his belt, and passed it to me in silence. It was one of those murderous, deep-bladed Albacete clasp-knives, for centuries a sinister speciality of this town. I prised the blade open from its sheath of horn, and the steel flushed red from the fire. Its glowing length was engraved in antique letters:

No me saques sin razon,
no me entres sin honor . . .

'Don't open without reason or close without honour,' said the Yank solemnly.

5

Tarazona de la Mancha

At last they sorted out a bunch of the greenest among us and put us in open lorries for Tarazona de la Mancha. This was the training camp for the 15th Brigade and lay some thirty miles across the plain to the north. It was the next leisured step in our preparation as fighting-men. Not one of us had fired a rifle, nor even held one as yet, but in Tarazona, they said, this would be seen to.

A half a dozen trucks took us over the frozen stream at La Gineta and humped us across the plateau. Sunlight blazed from the snow like an arctic summer, and blank umbrella pines stood darkly about. For once there was no wind, and although the air was freezing, we sang our way into the waiting town.

When we arrived we stopped singing. Tarazona de la Mancha looked hard and grim, a piece of rusted Castilian iron. The poverty of the snow-daubed hovels, huddled round the slushy square, gave an appearance of almost Siberian dejection. Squat, padded figures crept slowly about, each wrapped in a separate cocoon; and the harsh silence of the place and the people seemed to be sharing one purposeless imprisonment, where nothing soft, warm, tender or charitable could be looked for any more. This was a Spain stretched dead on a slab, a frozen cadaver, where, for all our early enthusiasms, we seemed to have come too late, not as defenders but as midnight scavengers.

Certainly Albacete had been shambles enough, but I remember the glazed astonishment in the eyes of my mates as we jumped off the lorries and gaped round the apparently empty and war-scalloped square. We were, in our forebodings, only half right; it seemed there was still some military life left in the town – up and down side-streets, in and out of the houses, soldiers came and went in ones and twos as though conducting some complicated domestic manoeuvres. Each was dressed in flamboyant rags which seemed to have designed themselves. Others carried baskets of potatoes, or bundles of wood, others broken pieces of furniture.

Some voice of authority we hadn't known we'd brought with us suddenly bawled at us to stand in line. An odd figure appeared, as though from a hole in the ground, said he was the Political Commissar, and addressed us briefly. I remember him well because, in spite of the cold, he was wearing only his pyjamas under a tattered poncho. He said we'd come

at the right moment, that victory was just round the corner, in our grasp, awaiting one final effort based on our ideological discipline. As he spoke he kept jumping up and down holding himself, like a little boy bursting to go to the lavatory. The man wore ragged odd slippers, and his toes were bare.

That was our welcome. We were then marched to our barracks, a back-street warehouse with ragged holes in the roof. We were stamped, listed, numbered, named, and each given a mint-new hundred peseta note. I looked at it in wonder, recalling my earlier days in this country, when five pesetas would last me the best part of a week. I stroked this finely engraved and watermarked piece of paper and thought of the princely excesses it might so recently have bought me. Wandering out through the town to see what the shops had to offer, I found only one, and it was selling beech nuts.

The central square in Tarazona must once have had some rough rusting elegance, but it was now badly battered by the fact of war. There'd been no fighting here, but the withdrawal of all normal life, together with a sudden revulsion for the past, had left their sickly marks everywhere. Chief sufferer, of course, was the ancient church, whose high-roofed edifice, hacked from red stone, now grimly haunted the plaza. The outside looked blind, blank and faceless, but the inside was now bare as a barn – the walls and little chapels cleared of their stars and images, the altar stripped, all the vestments gone. I couldn't help being reminded of our own Civil War, and of Cromwell's followers hatcheting the faces of the old stone saints, and stabling their horses in churches.

Now the inside of Tarazona's own church had an almost medieval mystery and bustle, an absence of holy silences and tinkling rituals, and a robust and profane reoccupation by the people. I found soldiers sleeping by the walls, under slashed and defaced icons, or sitting round flaming wood fires whose smoke drifted in clouds of shafted sunlight up to the smashed stained-glass windows under the roof. Here were arguments, singing, the perpetual boiling of water in cans, curses of men stumbling over sleeping figures, the high jangling of bells rung for sport or mischief, the sudden animal shriek of female laughter.

All over Republican Spain now such churches as this – which had stood for so long as fortresses of faith commanding even the poorest of villages, dominating the black-clad peasants and disciplining their lives and souls with fearsome liturgies, with wax-teared Madonnas and tortured Christs, tinselled saints and gilded visions of heaven – almost all were being taken over, emptied, torn bare, defused of their mysteries and powers, and turned into buildings of quite ordinary use, into places of common gathering.

But in this particular occupation of Tarazona's main church, I noticed something else. The soldiers who made free with these once holy spaces were a little more than normally loud and hearty, whereas the local villagers, who had perhaps regularly heard Mass here and spoken their darkest secrets in confession, now showed half-timid, half-shocked at what they were doing, and broke out at times into short bursts of hysteria like unchecked children amazed at their wantonness.

We spent the first evening mulling wine over a fire, anything to kill the taste. There was Doug, Danny and Brooklyn Ben, who had miraculously reappeared after his back-street mugging, cleansed of both bruising and political suspicion. Also Sasha, a towering White Russian from Paris and a newcomer to our company.

Danny had found some dried sausage which we fried on sticks. Huge shadows moved over the high arched ceilings, and flickered and died along the walls. We were uneasy; we still hadn't got used to the way of the village, to its almost brutal casualness and gloom. We didn't know yet what we were preparing for, or what was being prepared for us. As we drank the hot sour wine Sasha recited some poems of Mayakovsky, and Ben said they sounded

87

better in Yiddish. While they quarrelled, Danny sang some old music-hall songs in a cheerless adenoidal whine, till Doug covered his head with a blanket.

At last we left the Goyescan fires and smoke and half light of the church and went back to the freezing barracks. The guards sat hunched in the gateway, wrapped in balaclavas and ponchos, the late moon glinting on their bayonets. They didn't seem to care whether we were Moors or infidels. They merely burrowed down into the cold like dogs.

The barrack floor seemed to be covered with sleeping men, but we found a free space in the corner.

'By the way,' said Doug, as he settled down in the straw, 'I saw that lassie of yours today. You know, that wee one from Figueras. The one that kilt her father – or was it her grandfather? Aye, I dunno, but I just saw her riding down the street with a Captain.'

Before light next morning, I was awakened by the sound of a bugle – a sound pure and cold, slender as an icicle, coming from the winter dark outside. In spite of our heavy sleep and grunting longing for more, some of us began to love that awakening, the crystal range of the notes stroking the dawn's silence and raising one up like a spirit. There were certainly those who cursed the little bleeder, but the Brigade was proud of its bugler; he was no brash, brassy, spit-or-miss blaster of slumber, but one who pitched his notes carefully to the freezing stars and drew them out like threads of Venetian glass.

I got to know about him later. He was not exactly a soldier but a thirteen-year-old choirboy from Cuenca. Our Commander had heard him, kidnapped him, destroyed his papers of identity, and brought him as a pampered prisoner to Tarazona. One sometimes saw him by day, pretty as a doll, wriggling past in his outsize uniform. I spoke to him once, but he answered me in church Latin, eager to be left alone. Indeed, he seemed always to be alone, squirming quickly down side-streets or hurrying out to hide in the fields. It was only in the dark of dawn or at lights out, when he stood unseen at his post, that he was able to send out his frail and tenuous alarms.

After reveille came the brief luxury of lying awake, while those whose turn it was to do so brought round tin-drums of coffee brewed on fires in the snow outside. Ladled into our mugs, it had two cosy qualities: colour and warmth. Its flavour was boiler grease.

Terry, the company leader, a short, round, forty-year-old ex-NCO. from Swansea, began his

shouting around 6.30 a.m. He had learned an extraordinary, belligerent parade-ground patter which
he kept going in an abstract blood-curdling way
even when there was no one left in the room.

The company formed up in threes in the icy lane
outside, the big chaps in the front, the midgets
hidden in the rear, rather like a display on a green-
grocer's stall; then, after much shuffling, we
marched off to the plaza.

The morning parade was the only time when our
sad little village hardened and seemed to show some
purpose and strength. It was then that all the men
of the battalion came together from their various
nooks and grottoes, and stood under the red-
streaked morning sky before our neat and dim-
inutive Commander.

The lines of men were not noticeably impressive,
except that we displayed perhaps a harmonious gathering of oddities and a shared heroic daftness. Did
we know, as we stood there, our clenched fists raised
high, our torn coats flapping in the wind, and
scarcely a gun between three of us, that we had
ranged against us the rising military power of
Europe, the soft evasions of our friends, and the
deadly cynicism of Russia? No, we didn't. Though
we may have looked at that time, in our wantonly
tattered uniforms, more like prisoners of war than a
crusading army, we were convinced that we pos-

sessed an invincible armament of spirit, and that in
the eyes of the world, and the angels, we were on
the right side of this struggle. We had yet to learn
that sheer idealism never stopped a tank.

After parade came training in the snow – little fat
figures running and skipping about the fields, everyone padded up with cloaks and scarves like medieval
images from Brueghel. This medievalism spread to
the streets where off-duty soldiers sat round inter-
minable wood fires, or scampered about like children, making slides and playing snowball.

Doug, Sasha and I were drawn aside by the company leader and given a Maxim gun. We were told
to take it apart, clean it, put it together, fire it, and
generally get used to the thing. He thought we
would make a team; I don't know why. In an ice-
box cellar beneath the church, Doug and I took the
gun to pieces and Sasha reassembled it. First, second
and third time of firing, the Maxim jammed. The
giant Sasha cursed. Then Doug put it together, and
it fired. 'Sodding Russian,' he said, but Sasha was in
no way put out; he embraced Doug and gave him a
screw of tobacco.

That night we queued in the snow for food. The
day had been a hard one, and the food was late. We
sang and chanted in the lane outside the canteen,
banging our spoons and forks on our plates. The
food, when it came, was the usual heap of gritty

beans mixed with knobby pieces of livid meat. But there were no complaints; we were eating donkey, and we were eating better than most.

Then, I remember, a few days after coming to Tarazona, we got an early morning call for a Special Occasion. The bugles started about 5 a.m. There was a lot of shouting from Terry, and a certain excitement was transmitted. It was suggested we smarten ourselves up a bit, even shave for a change. A sack of new forage-caps, with tassels, were handed around, but after trying them on most of us threw them away.

They marched us, not to the parade-ground, but to the dark interior of the church and lined us up facing a platform half-obscuring the altar. We stood in wet, steaming rows, stamping our feet, and coughing. Electric light-bulbs were switched on, and tension mounted, while we glowered at the empty platform and grumbled.

Suddenly a little man jumped on to it, bouncy as a bull-calf, a minotaur in a short hairy coat, with a shiny half-bald head and piercing dark eyes under heavy commanding eyebrows.

'Comrades!' he cried. 'It is a special honour for me to stand before you at last — heroic defenders of democracy, champion fighters against the Fascist hordes . . .' It was Harry Pollitt, leader of the British Communist Party.

Where had he come from, I wondered, and what was he doing here at this hour? Dressed as it were for his King Street office, London, but standing before dawn by a church altar in La Mancha, for half an hour he held us in the grip of his fast, fist-jabbing oratory till he had us all standing with our arms raised, cheering. Pollitt had the true gift of a political leader of being able to rouse a cold and sullen mob, at six-thirty in the morning, by spraying them with short sharp bursts of provoking rhetoric till everyone was howling for victory. Pollitt's was a spare fighting style, calling us to fresh blood sacrifices, mass-solidarity, and other militant jousts of that order; but even his clichés were honed down to projectiles and pebbles for heroic slings.

I think we were astonished that this little man, exhausted from travelling and set down in this strange winter dawn, should pack such fire and fanaticism in him. He was my first experience of a professional working-class leader, who used words like street-calls and bugles. Wilting though we were, he had us convinced that not only would we smash Franco, Hitler and Mussolini, but go on to capture the whole world for the workers. We were all heroes, and he was our leader, and we cheered him as he stood there, larger than life, shining noble and shaking with emotion.

Then it was all over. The spell and magic quite

broken. He jumped down from the platform to mix with the men and was immediately surrounded by a jostling crowd. But not to slap him on the back or carry him in triumph through the town. No, they were plucking at his sleeves and pouring out their grievances, asking to be sent back home. 'It ain't good enough, you know. I bin out 'ere over nine months. Applied for leave and didn't get no answer. When they goin' to do something, eh, comrade? . . . eh? . . .' The last I saw of our morning Lucifer, he was backing towards the door, muted, expostulating, eyes groping for escape: 'Sorry, lads – sorry . . . nowt to do with me . . . sorry, I can't do owt about that . . .'

That night a young female voice spoke my name in the dark. I was walking near the church, and I'd thought there were no girls left in Tarazona. But the voice that called me had a familiar, hallucinatory echo. Doug was right; it was the 'wee lassie' from Figueras.

'Lorenzo – little Frenchman.'

'Eulalia!' I said.

She came and leant against me, threaded her small hand in mine and asked me to take her back to her lodging. She was working for the Socorro Rojo, she said . . . among other things. She knew I was here; a friend had told her. Had I killed any Fascists

yet? Ay! what a miracle it was to see me again –
'Lorenzo! – my little French brother . . .' 'English,' I
said stolidly. She nibbled at my sleeve. She seemed
to bind herself to me like a slim leather thong.

Her 'lodging' was a tiny, windowless room at the
top of an old house, empty save for a bed and some
posters. And a bottle of wine with two glasses standing near the head of the bed, and a man's great-coat
hanging on the back of the door.

Eulalia turned and smiled at me brilliantly, showing her tongue, her face cracking open like a brown
snake's egg hatching. Seen again in the pale light-
bulb, I'd forgotten how beautiful she was, small and
perilous, my murderous little dancer. She was
dressed in tight uniform that bit into her tiny waist.
She'd cut her hair short. She looked like a ten-year-
old boy.

She sat me down on the bed and poured me
some wine.

'Socorro Rojo,' she said. 'I heard they tried to
shoot you.'

'A mistake.'

'All the time they make mistakes!' She lifted my
hand with the glass towards my mouth. 'My poor
little brother. They don't shoot you now.'

'Later.'

'Perhaps later. Not now.'

In the pale cold light she quickly unzipped her

uniform, peeling off the crumpled green to reveal the strange pulsing fruit within. As soon as I was ready, she ran to fetch the man's great-coat from the door, helped me on with it, then wriggled inside. Burning cold she was, close as a second skin, her mouth running across my chest. In spite of the cold, I smelt her unforgettable smell, something I'd never known in anyone else – a mixture of fresh mushrooms and trampled thyme, woodsmoke and burning orange.

It didn't occur to me to wonder how such things could happen so easily, or to question the long and mysterious coincidence. At my age one was not surprised. Girls seen fleetingly, but memorably, from a train passing through Reading the wrong way, suddenly appeared at one's table in a London café. Or one whose face stopped one's heart as she got off a crowded bus in the City turned up days later sitting beside one in the cinema. Rare and magnetic driving patterns of youth, cutting across the humdrum chaos of multitudes.

So I found myself once more with the lyric-shaped girl, who had first held me without question in that far Figueras cellar, who had cried out her fears and hatreds in the ears of a stranger, and then disappeared in a flurry of kisses. Now, four hundred miles from there, she had casually reappeared in the night, in this beleaguered and sterile village, and here again she lay close against me, and I felt the anguished hunting of her hands, and heard again her familiar but incomprehensible whispers. All I understood her to say, in the last desperate throes of our night, was that she had found her father and brother, Lorenzo, little Frenchman, and would never lose sight of us ever again.

I got back to the barracks before anyone was awake, crawling through a hole in the wall beyond sight of the sentry. As I stretched out beside Doug he roused himself for a moment and said someone had been looking for me. He didn't know who it was, he said. Some boss from Albacete. Then he grunted and went to sleep again.

The next day, after a fumbling morning with the Maxim gun, I was called from my company and moved to 'special duties'. I don't know whether Sam, my old interrogator, had arranged it, or who, or why, but it became a secret and complicated little life. I was based, with a few others, in a small private house near the plaza. Few of our numbers were of the same nationality. Our leader, Kassell, was from Marseilles.

The house had pretty azulejo tiles on the floors and walls, tiny cold rooms, and Romano-Moorish pillars. It had probably belonged recently to a lawyer or doctor, to the son of a local land-owner,

even a priest. It was stripped bare now, except for its elegant proportions. We cooked for ourselves on brush fires, and slept on the floor.

There was a fragmented madness about our group, but it seemed to be necessary. Three of us spoke English, another three Spanish; but the lingua franca indeed was French. I won't attempt to detail the extent of our antics; they entailed meetings, reports, the issuing and signing for revolvers, notebooks, walking and stalking in twos. They also included covering-up, overlapping, watching, listening, and long hours wondering just what we were doing. Sometimes there were jovial evenings, fires burning, coñac and music, when we almost began to know each other. There were other times when we might doubt the purpose of our actions, and certainly when the means and the ends seemed squalid.

I can't, at this length of time, recall all the characters in the group; many are shapes in a shadow play only. I remember Kassell, the boss, thin as a peeled birch tree, with a starved face and feverish eyes. We had Emile, a Dutch professor, hunched and bearded; peachy-cheeked Rafael, a horse-breaker from Jaen; two tiny Belgians – Jean and Pip – agile and feminine as lemurs; and a dark, silent Catalan we nicknamed Compadre, who may once have been a monk.

I had arrived late in Tarazona, and found it in

turmoil, no longer simply a base for the International Brigades. Politically and physically its battalions were dispersing or dead, and a deliberate new nationalism was taking over. Those ragged ranks, once packed with the innocents and scatterings of Britain and Europe, were now being officially stiffened by troops from the Republican Army – Basques, Catalans, Gallegos, Castillanas, Valencianas, even Mallorquins. In such a pivotless mêlée our group found its natural home, and could operate without guide or comment.

I recall one little job, just before Christmas, but still can't swear to its reality or purpose. Kassell called us together in one of the inner rooms of the house and passed round a photograph telling us to memorize it carefully. It was of a slight, round-shouldered youth, with dark fruity lips and the wide dream-wet eyes of a student priest or poet. His brow was smooth and babyish, his long chin delicately pointed.

Kassell told us his story – improbable for such a face. A rich Mallorquin, it seemed, son of a Count, he was also a hero of the Barcelona risings. A gunman, dynamiter, he'd executed three leading Trotskyists, been kidnapped, tortured and sentenced to death. He'd escaped and come south, had been seen in Albacete, and it was believed he was on his way here.

'Why here?' asked Emile.

'He knows he'll be safe with us,' said Kassell.

The two little Belgians looked at each other.

'What's his name?' asked the Dutchman.

'Who knows?' said Kassell. 'Could be anything.' He turned over the photograph. 'But it says "Forteza" here.'

So Forteza we called him, and we went out to start our search – first to watch the morning camiones coming in. I paired up with Rafael, and together we scrutinized each newly arrived face while pretending to be listing numbers and counting heads. The trucks lurched to a halt in the square, their bonnets steaming, the men dropping off them like clods of mud. A mix of spiritless faces passed before us in the bleared light: white, hungry, blank – Anglo-Saxon, Slav, Latin-French, Iberian. But no sign or shade of Forteza.

For two days we met all the camiones, checked the church and barracks and outlying billets. Then the second night Kassell called us together. 'He's here,' he said, his face soft with concern, 'but not wishing to show himself.' Our job was still to find him, quickly before someone else did, and so give him our protection. Forteza was young, valuable, dangerous and hunted – but he'd also lost his nerve. If he falls into the wrong hands, Kassell was saying . . .

I remember staring bemused at the pretty tiles on the walls, half-drowsing in the warmth of the wood fire. Kassell's voice went smoothly on; Rafael sat on the floor, sorting and soaking beans; Emile, hunched and cross-legged, scribbled in the margin of a book; Jean and Pip played at pocket chess. All of us seemed to be waiting for something, but at the same time were relaxed and cosy.

Suddenly there was a muffled knock at the door, and Kassell went to answer it. When he returned his face had a curious tight radiance about it. He took Rafael aside, and they looked at me, then Rafael beckoned, and threw me a heavy coat. Before we left, he led me through the kitchen where we drank a couple of glasses of coñac each.

It was after midnight when we set out together in a fine and freezing darkness. Rafael began muttering obscenities that seemed more pointed and personal than the usual flow of Spanish rhetorical oaths. Tarazona was without lights, but the stars were big and fierce. This wasn't a patrol; Rafael knew exactly where he was going; and so, with a chill certainty, did I.

We came quite soon to an alleyway which even in the starlight I recognized by the peculiar winding of its walls. I knew the darkened house we entered, and the flapping wood on the stairs. I knew the sagging door on which we knocked.

Eulalia was not surprised to see us. She had obviously been waiting some while. She held a candle to our faces and turned and nodded towards the bed. She was in her tight, trim overalls, and wore a scarf round her head. 'Venga, Rubio,' she said to me.

On her rumpled bed, shaking with fear or fever, was the youth we instantly recognized from the photograph, except that the once smooth face of the priestlike dreamer was now savagely and bitterly scarred. When he saw Rafael and me, he shrank back on the bed, doubled up, and drew his knees to his chin. He broke into a paroxysm of coughing, while Eulalia soothed him, and wrapped a ragged blanket round him.

We sat down on the bed and waited for him to stop coughing. He coughed like a little dog. Eulalia stood by the door, her long eyes shining with candle-light, but they were no longer the whispering eyes I knew.

'Frenchman,' she said, and jerked her head sharply. Rafael cursed and laid his hand on my knee. 'We could carry him,' he said. 'He's only a baby. Anyway, he's got to come.'

Forteza grew quiet, then pulled himself into a sitting position. He asked if we had any coñac. Rafael was carrying a flask, and gave him some, which he drank in little birdlike sips. Then he smiled and let us draw him to his feet. Rafael grew hearty and wrapped his arm round Forteza's shoulders. 'We were worried about you, man,' he said, guiding him towards the door. 'For God, why d'you take such risks?'

I saw the panic slowly fade from Forteza's eyes as he struggled to find his balance. Eulalia lightly touched the back of his neck, then put her cold hand to my cheek. 'He could be you, little brother,' she said. We helped the lad down the stairs and supported him through the streets. Forteza's skeletal frame between us was as light as a bundle of sticks.

When we got him back to the house, Kassell was drinking coffee by the fire. Jean and Pip left their chess game, the Dutchman stopped writing, and all joined Rafael and me by the door. Then Kassell got up and strode forward, crinkling in his black leather mackintosh, threw his arms round Forteza and kissed him.

Forteza stood quiet, neither shivering nor coughing now. 'Welcome, comrade,' said Kassell, with his watery smile. 'We thought something bad had happened to you.' He ran his hands quickly over the boy's thin body and led him into the inner room. Jean and Pip returned to their chess game, and the Dutchman to his writing. A little later we heard the sound of a shot.

6

The Tarazona Trap

We spent most days now just watching and waiting; watching each other and waiting for the war to move. It was a festering time, drenched in doubt and suspicion. The Republic was in peril, and one took no risks with its enemies. But of the several dark little games in which Kassell involved us, few of them seemed to bear the stamp of reason, and the authority behind them, if any, was a mystery. One hoped, yet doubted, that they had a purpose, but as in most wars they were bungled and malevolent jokes.

One day Rafael and I were told to go and track down an old farmer who lived out in the wasteland towards Madrigueras. There'd been some small acts of sabotage – a couple of lorries blown up, part of a bridge destroyed – and the old man was thought responsible. He'd been seen by a neighbour packing long sticks of dynamite into a box, so we were told simply to go out and get him.

It was a cold walk through the snow, and for once Rafael had no coñac. He smoked instead, using the dry edge of a newspaper wrapped round a small bundle of herbs. Rafael would smoke anything: old beech leaves, sugared-moss, corn-husks, even crushed pine bark with tar – at least that was the smell of it. For cigarette papers he preferred foreign journals – *Paris Soir* or *L'Humanité* – or the thin pages of antique prayer-books.

'These amateur dynamiters are the worst,' said Rafael. 'And where did he get the stuff? Not by parachute, that's for sure. We need it, anyway. And him.'

We came to the farm in the late afternoon. There was a thicket of thorn bushes round it, and a leashed demented dog. The brushwood roofs of the buildings were held down by heavy stones and the light on the walls was a sort of dimpled pewter. We saw no horses, mules or donkeys – we'd probably eaten the lot in Tarazona.

We dodged the dog and approached the buildings. A short thin woman came to the door and saw our guns. She smothered the fierce flash in her eyes and told us the house was ours. 'Come in. There is only the old one,' she said. The howling wolf-dog leapt to the full extent of his chain, clawing the air, his wet teeth shining like ice.

We went into the small bare room and found the dynamiter standing ready, black hat in hand, dressed in his best corduroy suit.

'Mario Nuñez, at your service,' he said.

'It's lies,' cried the woman, walking angrily up and down, bobbing jerkily as though riding a miniature bicycle.

The farmer stood with bowed head, resigned and waiting.

'It's a lie – a lie!' the woman cried again.

Rafael shouldered his rifle and said it was time to go. The farmer raised a long brown hand and brushed the woman lightly across the forehead, and for a moment they stood motionless together in the bare luminous room, like two age-worn wooden carvings.

Outside, a car blew its horn, and we led the farmer through the door. Emile and Jean were waiting to take him to Albacete. There was much, it was thought, that the dynamiter could tell us. Meanwhile, Rafael and I had to search the place.

The woman followed us as we returned to the house.

'What do you want, you pollutions?' she asked.

'Only the dynamite, grandmother,' said Rafael.

'You're as likely to find the Holy Virgin as dynamite here,' said the woman.

'That I believe,' said Rafael.

We searched, but found very little in the house. Only a picture of Saint Teresa and the Prime Minister, Azaña Largo Caballero, on the walls and some rolled-up mats and a wooden bowl on the floor. How could this man have been a saboteur, or even dangerous at all? Yet he'd been seen packing dynamite in a box.

We went into the yard and examined the outhouse. The woman followed us like a strutting hawk. The building was of crumbling mud-brick, the thatch breaking away in the wind. Bits of harness lay around, and the remains of a cart, and some olive stones in a broken barrel. Rafael began stamping the floor and eventually he found it – a mouldering trap-door fitted with an iron ring.

'Ojala!' said Rafael, and lifted it open. We climbed down the ladder into the small dark cellar below, lit a match, and saw a padlocked chest. Then the old hawk struck, flew down the ladder behind us and began clawing at us with her long black nails.

While she fought, she cursed us and all our families. Then she turned and threw herself across the chest. I remember her tattered black clothes splayed from her arms and legs, reminding me of a shot crow hung up on a fence. So that's where it was. Rafael lifted the now exhausted woman and set her down in the corner, where she remained bolt upright, weeping.

We kicked the padlock from the chest and opened the lid. In the dim light we saw the long white sticks stacked neatly together. Dozens and dozens of them. Rafael crowed. 'Mother of God! The cunning old devil. Enough here to blow up an army.' Breathing heavily, and with great care, he lifted a stick in his hands. It fell in two parts, each joined by a thread. The sticks of dynamite were long altar candles which the old farmer was holding in trust for the church. Together with some items of priests' regalia hidden away at the bottom of the trunk. Pandering to the priesthood was thought by many of us at that time to be as bad as blowing up our bridges.

Quite soon, and without explanation, I was dropped from Kassell's little outfit and switched to another company. I don't know whether I'd passed a test or simply been discarded, but it was back to the ranks for me. No longer the feminine little house with its tiny balconies, the shadowy evenings by the wood fire, the privileged suppers with Kassell rehearsing his macabre and amorphous exercises.

He shook my hand when I left.

'None of us are specialists,' he said vaguely. 'We can't afford specialists in this war. We must follow the struggle wherever it leads us.'

My new Company Commander was Polish-American and wore a Siberian hat. He had a beautiful absent face and a drowsy manner that quite swallowed up his authority, so that one frequently lost sight of him for hours together, only to find him perhaps marching in the rear of the ranks carrying somebody else's kit. Comrade Caplin believed in equality to the point of personal self-effacement.

I'd been in the company for several days, packed at night in a warehouse with some hundred others, when the word came that we'd been found new billets. We paraded leaderless in the plaza, stamping our feet while the search began for Caplin. He was found in the cinema, writing poetry, and he came and led us out of the town.

He took us to a gaunt little chapel on the edge of a hill, an old, beautifully proportioned, but crumbling building which was, it seemed, to be our new headquarters. The heavy main door had been ripped from its hinges and now leant half-burnt against the wall.

The interior of the chapel was wrecked and gutted. Nothing remained but some small empty niches and the bare, naked altar. As we stamped in from the slushy street, our clothes and ponchos soaking, each man bagged his personal patch of ground by throwing down his kit. The chapel filled rapidly, the territories staked out; but I hesitated as under a spell. The altar, beneath its tinted east window, was a stripped pedestal of stone and plaster lightly washed in flaking blue paint. Quickly I went up to

it, threw down my bags, stretched myself along it, and lit a cigarette. With this gesture, this idiot impulse of brash bravado, I believe I stained the rest of my life . . .

Half the members of my new company were Spanish now – stocky, grinning, round-headed types from the villages north of Madrid. Although young, their faces had that wizened, russet-apple texture that came from exposure to fierce winters and roasting summers. When they saw me claim the altar for my bed, some of them looked at me with blank, frozen stares, while others flashed their teeth and chanted crude parodies of the litany.

But for most, even the most ribald, profane and godless, there seemed to be an invisible area here which it was still impossible to cross without the blessing of a priest. Even in this bare and mutilated chapel a holy charm seemed to lie on the ground surrounding the sacred stone. An unseen line ran from wall to wall and everyone appeared content to remain behind it. Except for me, the petty violator.

The chapel soon took on a humid male cosiness, while the ghostly aura of incense which had impregnated the walls was quickly obliterated by our musky presence. We plugged the doors and broken windows against the heavy cold. We built up a thick atmosphere of smoke and coffee; we talked, played cards and quarrelled. There was nothing to do. A great pause, a great silence had settled on Tarazona. In the snows of the sierras the battle for Teruel had begun, a last desperate attempt to cut off Franco's north-eastern salient which threatened to slice our territory in two. For the sake of pride, politics and the people's morale, only Spanish Republican troops were being used in this attack. The International Brigade was temporarily set aside; indeed, it was hoped officially it would not be needed at all.

So at this time, when the frozen peaks were aflame and the slow bloody encirclement of Teruel city began, we just lay around in our smoky chapel, waiting as Christmas came.

We had one true veteran among us, the only one with battle experience, and he showed it with a moody lassitude and a quiet indifference to discipline. Arturo, from Bilbao, was the company machine-gunner, weedy and strangely tall for a Basque. His was the long recumbent figure I saw every morning stretched out near the altar steps. After the breakfast bucket of coffee had gone round, he would remain for hours lying spread on the floor, rigid, motionless, like a medieval stone relic, while his cadaverous face flickered with fever. Someone found a priest's robes in the chapel cellars and these Arturo wrapped round himself. He'd then lie stiffly cocooned in scarlet and black, cursing and shivering.

Our company leader by this time had lost himself. There were no parades or drill; we ruled ourselves. Sometimes Arturo would rise up, throw off his robes, assemble his machine-gun, and blow great holes in the walls. This raised our spirits, and under Arturo's instructions we formed teams and did it ourselves. The din in the long narrow chapel was ear-blasting, but we were pleased with our training; it was all we got.

At night especially, under the string of light-bulbs, I think there was a simplicity about us. Some new Americans and British had joined our company. Wine was brought in, and we began to use the altar as a kind of bar. We were young and, as I remember, direct and trusting, even in our fights and excesses. Among us the young Spanish peasant, American student, Welsh miner, Liverpool dock-worker had met on a common shore.

We didn't talk about it much, during those days of waiting. I played chess with Paul, a scholarly mechanic from Ohio, whose dark trembling earnestness concealed a sharp Jewish wit. We were restless, moody, charged for action. Girls came whispering at the door and the chapel windows. Stubby little virgins, with wide liberated eyes. They stood waiting outside, in solemn groups of two. They would go with us anywhere, into farm huts and hovels. But none would cross the threshold of our sacred building.

An almost wolf-like hunger, too, was now part of our lives, sharpened by the winter cold and idleness. At last, wearying of our acorn coffee and thin donkey soup, a half a dozen of us pooled our pay – over a thousand pesetas in fresh-printed notes – and persuaded an old farmer to part with three chickens, each of which looked as hungry as we were. These bony birds we took to two widowed sisters who lived with their old father on the other side of the town. They had one of those bare stone kitchens which were still almost medieval – a paved floor, high roof, brick and tiled stove by the wall, a few chairs, a table, a twist of olive wood in the corner, and hanging from the rafters an old ham-bone and some harness.

The sisters were wispy, watchful, bright-eyed, sunken-cheeked, their bodies almost mummified in their widow-black. The father sat on a high-backed chair near the stove, his limbs as lean as a whippet's. He slipped to his tiny feet as we came crowding in and raised a wrinkled fist.

'Your house,' he said. 'José, at your service. And my daughters – Doña Anselm – Doña Luisa . . .'

115

The sisters bridled at this, but lost none of their watchfulness. They took the birds we had brought with us with little clucks of the tongue. 'Come back in two hours,' they said.

So we walked around in the snow, and when we returned Doña Anselm swept our boots with a broom. The old stove blazed with a mixture of wood and refuse, and a great iron pot stood bubbling upon it. The entire kitchen simmered and was awash with steam, a steam banked on the long-forgotten juices of real home-cooked food, swimming aromas of tomatoes, dried beans, and garlic sausage, and boiled chicken peeling on the bone. How the widows had done it seemed a miracle. We stood there in a swoon of hunger. A hunger more blest in that it was about to be appeased. The widows could have asked us another thousand pesetas.

I'd been hungry before, and had also known the simple, voluptuous appetite of youth when taste was never jaded. I remember as a boy being so in love with bread and butter and the cloudy meat of a new-boiled egg that I could hardly wait to go to sleep at night so that morning breakfast should come again. So it seemed now, that long moment of delayed consummation, as we sat round the table while the sisters fussed and quarrelled by the stove and carried us at last the stew in a great earthen dish. We had brought our slabs of grey bread, our

metal knives and spoons, and the plates we had
were of curved polished wood. The farmer's three
birds, who must have been survivors of at least two
long winters, now swam brokenly in a thick soup
of beans and sausage, splendidly recharged with suc-
culence. Doña Anselm guarded the dish while her
sister spooned out our portions, one squashed steamy
limb to each plate.

A jar of thin reedy wine was passed around, a
brew strangely flavoured with sage and cinnamon –
a lacy, fastidious old woman's drink which hinted
at secluded and secret comforts.

'Eat!' snapped Doña Anselm, and we broke our
grey bread with solemn ritual under her scaring
eyes. Six young strangers at their private table, for
whom they had cooked three old and irreplaceable
hens; we were guests, visitors, but also the enemy in
possession. The sisters clearly took no sides in this
war, which had occupied their land and must be
endured. They served but did not join us as we
plunged into our food, while the old man by the
stove stared at the floor and waited.

Lopez, a late arrival, and the only Spaniard among
the six of us, set himself up as a surrogate host.

'Three in one pot,' he said, beaming round at us
proudly. 'Few of you could have eaten better.'

Carried away by the majesty of the moment, he
began to pick out pieces from the dish with his

stubby fingers and hand them to us with a bow. Doña Anselm hit him with a spoon.

'What are you doing?' she cried. 'Have some culture, man.'

'At my brother's wedding,' said Lopez, 'we had two birds and a rabbit – stewed in wine. I have never forgotten.'

Doña Luisa sniggered. 'Yes. The bride, the bride's mother and the groom.'

Lopez lowered his face to his plate. We others were now deep in our meal, skewering, spooning, using our fingers, awash with flavours and greed. Few of us, I think, had been long from home; none of us, except perhaps Lopez, were married. Instead of great chunks of swede and donkey thrown into a rusty bucket and boiled by some lout in the barrack bath-house, we were now eating food prepared by the hands of women, especially and particularly for us.

In reality, it must have been a poor and scratch-me-down meal. But it was a memorable banquet in that winter of war. In the end it cost each of us several weeks' pay. We were bullied, cursed, perhaps even despised by the sisters, but we were not cheated. There was enough on the stove for all of us. Sprawled at the table, feet up, near repletion, chasing the pimply chicken skins through the thinning soup, digging out the last bits of sausage with our bread, we wallowed now, wheedled more wine, sipped it slowly and grew sentimental. As the afternoon passed, even the sisters softened a little, and found us some beech nuts and raisins.

We gave them the rest of our money, and the old man in the corner said, 'Now you'll be able to buy that clock.'

When we'd finished all there was, we sang, sleepy-eyed, while the sisters cleared the table and put all the chicken bones on a plate and set them down on the old man's lap. Slowly, one by one, he picked them up and passed them between his naked gums, dwelling on each with a delicate bliss as though he was sucking asparagus. He had waited five hours for this moment and now his time had come. He tasted his portion of bones with the absorbed grace of a prince.

Christmas was on us, and the wind blew from the north with a cutting edge of pain. The gritty snow was pretty and pitiless. We fetched cartloads of wood from out of the countryside, chopping down century-old olives to build up our fires. In our state of mind, I don't think there was one among us who wouldn't have burnt a rare church carving, relic of a thousand years' piety, to have gained himself five minutes' warmth.

Gradually news from the front was ferried down

from the sierras, news we could scarcely believe. Launched in one of the worst winters in Spanish memory, in one of Spain's coldest, remotest mountains, our Army, without artillery and at the height of a blizzard, had attacked and surrounded the city of Teruel, and was even said to be fighting in the streets. After the remorseless decline and atrocious defeats of the summer, we had at last a hope to believe in. Slowly, bloodily, month after month, Franco's forces had been sopping up Spain, pushing our lines back towards the eastern coast. Now we were aimed at a forward city, at a point of greatest threat and danger. People talked now of tides turning, and paths to victory reopening at last.

Yet in Tarazona, in the silence, the cold idleness of our lives, crouched around in our ponchos, cleaning and re-cleaning our guns, we thought of the hundred thousand fighting our war in those mountains, and wondered what this training camp was for.

In this silence, Christmas came, muted, inglorious, and small Red Cross parcels were passed among us, some from Britain and some from France. On Christmas Day I tasted, with almost erotic excitement, a twopenny bar of Cadbury's Milk Chocolate, and smoked a shilling packet of Players. I was as affected as much by the piercing familiarity of their flavours as by the homely reassurance of their wrappings.

120

Then I remember the see-saw of news, reports and rumours. A van-driver arrived seeking a supply of blankets. It had taken him three days to cover the hundred miles from the front. Here was no hero or victorious eagle but a shivering and ragged man. He told us of pain and snow-blindness, panic and exposure on the road, while his eyes jumped like beans in his head. Oh, yes, we were winning in Teruel. He'd seen the dead stacked like faggots of wood round the walls. Frozen barricades of flesh you could shelter behind, protected from the wind and bullets. He'd seen mules drop dead in the cold, then set stiff and rigid in the road so that they held up the traffic and had to be sawn up in solid blocks and removed. His tales were of a reversal of hell, and he seemed as astonished by them as were his hearers; that he, a Spaniard, had seen such weather in his own country, such acts of slaughter in death's own climate, and the young soldiers, even alive, dressed in sheeted white.

As we listened to this pop-eyed, half-demented man, something of our secure camp Christmas went away. It was as if he'd opened a door and admitted a blast of arctic and charnel house, wiped the frost from our cabin window and shown us the wolves.

A few days later, a quite different messenger turned up: Bill Rust, the editor of the *Daily Worker* — a dapper, soft-spoken, rather chummy man, wearing a dark London overcoat and a warm felt hat. I remember having seen him a few weeks earlier, on his way through Albacete, his face tense with anxiety and exhaustion. Now he had a pink glowing look of half-suppressed triumph, like a football manager whose team had just won the cup.

Teruel had fallen, he told us; the mountain fortress was ours, and he'd walked in the liberated streets of the city. To prove it, he showed us the inside of his hat. On the sweat-band it said: Sombreros de Teruel.

It was, it seemed, his only loot. Modest as ever, he'd picked it out of a broken shop window. There was some rejoicing that night. Rust's tale of that victory was perhaps our most hopeful moment of the winter – for most even the best in the war.

Then, in the beginning of the new year, all news of victory ceased. In fact, there was suddenly no news at all. Our soldiers, first one or two, and then in companies, began silently to disappear from the town. One morning I woke to find that more than half my friends had gone. I never saw them again.

7

Radio Madrid

Early in January I was ordered to go to Madrid, which rather surprised me as I'd been expecting to be sent elsewhere. The order was passed on from the Political Commissar, and came from Captain Sam of Albacete, who apparently had not forgotten me.

He wanted me to go, together with himself and some others, to make a few broadcasts from Madrid Radio to America. This was the capital's second winter of front-line war, beleaguered, half-besieged, and stuck like a fist in Franco's mouth and crammed fast against his teeth.

A dozen of us took off just after dawn, packed in an open truck. We were a mixed lot, and I couldn't believe all of us were going to make short-wave broadcasts; some, by the look of them, were on more solemn errands. We sat on wooden boxes at the back of the truck, and waited for the dawn landscape to lighten. It was flat, frosty, with umbrella pines on the horizon, like dirty paper fastened down with pins.

We had a hundred and fifty miles of this vacant country to cross, a straight melancholy road scoring the sterile La Mancha, with no mark of man save a few broken windmills. As we bumped slowly along, I thought again of the huge emptiness of this country, where, apart from cramped slums of the still medieval cities, raised on crusts of imperial and religious splendour, there remained little more than the untenable plains and vertical deserts of the sierras, yielding to and supporting no one.

The road was bare save for a few sleepy road-blocks; though one was less sleepy than the others and was manned by a heavily armed anarchist who stopped our truck and objected to Captain Sam's cap, saying it wasn't sufficiently democratic. But Sam, with a few key phrases and his cold clear smile, sent the vigilante scurrying off with apologies.

Passing through Mola de Cuervo we had a burst tyre, but this caused us no difficulty either. Our driver simply went up to another truck, parked unattended by the church, walked round it slowly, removed the wheel he wanted, and left a receipt, signed by Sam, on the windscreen.

For the rest of the journey Harry and Bill, two Glaswegian veterans of the Aragon front, played cards on a board and quarrelled dramatically in a slurred incomprehensible accent. A couple of Spanish comrades, with long Cordobese faces, dozed sitting upright like Easter Island gods. Another soldier, I think he was Dutch, played for several hours a series of monotonous airs on the harmonica – that tinned exhalation of all the boredom of war.

Captain Sam had been busy scribbling notes on his knee. We went over them together, suspicious and watchful. I added a few bits of my own, and smiling Sam cut them out. This was to be the script for our broadcast tonight.

As the afternoon darkened we entered the suburbs of the city, threading close to the enemy lines. There was little to be seen: rotting sandbags, broken roads, barricades of brick and bedsteads, shuttered windows, closed shops and bars.

I'd known Madrid briefly in the summer before the war, when it had a light air of penurious, unassuming fiesta. Now with siege and winter, the skies had come down, and as we neared the centre of the city, passing through the cloaked guards of the road-blocks, the streets seemed empty save for bent hurrying figures, wrapped in blankets, making their way home.

We found, however, a quite cushy spot for the night. We were billeted in a small gypsy hotel just off the Calle Echegarry, near to the Puerta del Sol. Ramon, our Asturian driver, camped out on the cobbles under his truck – just to keep it in the family, he said. The hotel was run by a committee, who welcomed us at a table in the hall, and gave out meal tickets accompanied by clenched raised salutes. We sat round the dining-room, at first cowed and prim, like orphan children awaiting our institutional soup. But the meal, when it came, though poor, was ribald, and served by rollicking militia-girls. They had the dark physical power that Spanish girls are conscious of early, with small jungly bodies, split olive eyes, and voices like laser beams. They wore blue baggy overalls, but so tightly belted at the waist, and deeply slashed at the throat, they appeared to have arisen half-naked from tumbled beds.

Only Captain Sam seemed unaware of the erotic atmosphere of the place, as he sat head down, dashing off manifestos on the table-top, a bent cheroot in his mouth. He, and a couple of black-smocked old men, probably delegates from some distant village commune, who remained in stiff formal silence, skin tightly wrapping their cheekbones, rough hands gripping their knees.

Otherwise I remember the noise, the near frenzy, in that basement dining-room, that winter night, in the heart of besieged Madrid; the war posters on the walls with their flat, cut-out heroes and their slogans of arousal, defiance, hope; the plates of ordinary steamed potatoes, many of them black with frost;

the cheeky militia-girls twisting nimbly among the groping hands of the soldiers; and the soldiers, foul-mouthed, grabbing at girls and food, and grinning around them with vacuous pleasure.

Here were young veterans and half-trained new-comers, combatants but a short bus-ride from the front, those who had slipped past death and returned, and those who must very soon die; a few officers, agents, spies, touts and journalists – all who found in this cellar in this huge dark city an incongruous moment of temporary comfort.

After supper Captain Sam called me up to his room, where I found two dramatically dissimilar persons crouched over a table nodding and chanting in broken English. One was bald and round as a Michelin tyre man, the other slim and pretty as a schoolgirl. Spread before them on the table were two half-eaten tomatoes, some crumbling dried fish, and an English translation of Machado, which both were intoning.

Sam introduced us: the round man, Esterhazy, an Austrian writer; the pretty youth, Ignacio, ex-student of English and Arabic at the University of Salamanca.

'Tell us the accent!' cried Esterhazy, waving to me. 'Come along, comrade, instruct us, please!'

Sam said my accent was terrible, even he couldn't

understand it. Nevertheless, we rehearsed the poem, which they were going to broadcast together that night, in chorus, and taking alternate verses.

Ignacio was most rousing, even feminine, speaking as it were below the waist, his voice slender, flesh-warm and caressing, his eyes changing shadow with every line. Billowing Esterhazy, meanwhile, provided the windy brass-section, grunting and blaring beneath the other's treble.

In the end, they built up a fine duet between them, swaying together at the littered table, while Sam and I worked out the rest of the programme which was made up of chatty interviews, propaganda and 'culture'.

Our first short-wave broadcast was timed for midnight, and theoretically beamed to East Coast America. It was planned as a beleaguered, backs-to-the-wall, defiant call for help; and some of those things it certainly turned out to be.

A couple of armed militiamen picked us up about eleven, their job to guide us through the streets to the radio station. We'd drunk several bottles of wine by then and considered ourselves well rehearsed, and we swaggered out through the dim-lit hall. The streets were almost deserted – no traffic, a distant cry, a few late footfalls of the night, the wind from the sierras lightly ruffling the shutters.

Sam told us to stick close to the militiamen and, if challenged, to freeze. We moved by the faint glimmer of oil-lamps shining under the curtains of doorways, by the thin glow of starlight on the edge of the rooftops. The air was as cold as mile-high Madrid could be. Sam shivered and swore. Esterhazy blew self-comforting bubbles in his cheeks. The militiamen coughed and spat. From the next street came a shout and the sound of running feet. Young Ignacio gripped my arm.

'I am a poet,' I remember him saying. 'I don't wish to be here. I belong to music and song, not war.'

We had left the city centre and were stumbling down side-streets, when one of the militiamen tripped up and cursed. A shadowy bundle lay on the pavement, a bundle that gave a weak, old cry. The soldier lit a match. 'You can't sleep here, grandmother. If you try to sleep here, you'll die.'

We knocked at a nearby door, and roused a trembling couple, who lit a candle while we carried the old soul inside.

The wife recognized her with a cry, and said she used to run a kiosk in the square; it was her home, but it had just recently been destroyed by a shell.

'They fall at all times, as you know. Both night and day. We are none of us safe, before God.' Distraught and whining, she clutched at her throat and threw a helpless glance at her husband.

'Dead by our door. The shame of it! How shall we face the world?'

The husband told her not to be stupid, and said he would fetch a hand-cart in the morning and wheel the old woman to hospital. He peered at us nervously, then raised his hand. 'Go with God,' he said. 'And long live the Republic!'

Now it was late, and we hurried on to the next road-block, which was under a railway bridge. It was heavily armed, but no one knew the password, not even our guides, or Sam. We saw the gleam of teeth, the glitter of bayonets, and heard the jaunty cocking of rifles. Then suddenly one of the sentries cried, 'Aren't you Rocio?' and one of our soldiers said, 'Yes.' They were fishermen from the same village, were brought up together, but, judging from their conversation, didn't like each other much. But they let us through, stumbling over tins and stones, accompanied by jolly in-bred insults.

The broadcasting studio was in a dank dark basement in a Victorian-style tenement. As we stumbled down the stairs, stepping over heaps of refuse, the building throbbed and snored with sleepers of all ages, most of the rooms having been set aside for soldiers' families.

Sam led us to a cramped little room stuffed with coils and valves, where a young blond announcer, sweating in his shirt-sleeves, read a war communiqué in Teutonic English. He winked at Sam as we entered and nodded towards a table, around which we grouped ourselves. Finally, from this tiny cell in Madrid, fumed by wine and tobacco smoke, we went into our broadcast – three thousand miles across the winter seas. Who could be listening, I wondered – truck-drivers sealed in their cabs, young radio hams skimming the air-waves, bored barmen and husbands seeking the evening sports news, widows in Long Island mansions awaiting their lovers?

I doubt that they could, or would, or did. Sam took the mike and read out the manifesto we had stitched up together, ending with a list of names of some Lincoln Brigade heroes. As a climax we had planned to play a few bars of the 'Internationale', but we mixed up the labels and put on 'The Skater's Waltz' instead. But I had a feeling that we could not be heard at all, that the microphones were simply not connected to anything, that this was all a panto-mime to placate the gods.

Nevertheless, we kept on with it. Esterhazy and Ignacio took their turn, and droned and fluted into their prepared Machado. I don't know what the effect of an obscure Spanish poem, in a bad English translation, delivered in unison by a booming Aus-trian and a nervous young Madriléno, would have on an uncertain audience thousands of miles away, but one doubted that it would command their single-minded attention or cause them much stirring of the breast.

Not that Sam's and my contribution was any more compelling. We had worked out an interview in which Sam questioned me about the volunteer routes across the Pyrenees. This had seemed easy and matter of fact enough when we rehearsed it earlier that evening, but once returned to the microphone, in this more casual role, Sam's personality suffered a cardinal breakdown – gone was the urbane propagandist, the donnish debater, the merciless interrogator of spies and traitors, the ice-cold political killer – suddenly I was confronted with an oily and unctuous crawler, and this fawning Sam was an unsettling experience.

The unreality disappeared when the shelling began, somewhere about three in the morning. We heard it first as a distant metallic bark, honed and polished by the freezing air, followed by an indrawn silence, a rapidly approaching whine, then the brief uproar of exploding masonry. Curiously, these sounds then seemed to fall back on themselves, receding in waves of silence, shouts, running feet, and finally in distant cries.

The first shell broke some glass, shook the studio walls, juggled the furniture, and brought down some dust. The engineer signalled to us to go on, and this we did, and at last the broadcast seemed to make some sense. We began to talk together in normal voices, to ask each other why we were here. Captain Sam's face returned to its original protean calm. His back straightened and he reclaimed his authority. With several minute intervals, both near and far, the shells continued to fall. The studio door opened and a group of women came in, carrying bundles of sleeping or whimpering children. Each of the women's faces had that pallor of patience and hunger as though they had been rubbed in damp grey ashes. They bowed to us apologetically, hesitated a moment, then sank in a circle around the walls. If we have to die, let us die where there is light, among each other, and near the power of these men talking a kind of Latin, like priests.

So in this cramped semi-basement in the beleaguered city, surrounded by our cloaked, fugitive audience, and to its background of shuffles, sighs and murmurs, and the occasional spiked thud of explosions outside, we talked on, read poems, swinging the microphone between us, while the large frightened eyes of the women stared up at our mouths as if we were conjuring for them, in our foreign tongues, magic spells, incantations and prayers.

Some time later the German announcer suddenly handed me a battered violin, with an old bow like

an unravelled horsewhip. At the sight of the instrument faces softened, eyes brightened, sleeping children were awoken with pinches. 'Musica! . . . musica!' the whisper went round. And I saw again those expressions of gentle pleasure and anticipation that I'd known in poor Spanish villages before the war.

I didn't play much, the strings were frayed and greasy, but I scratched away at some old Spanish dances which I'd learnt on my previous visit, and I played them as loud and as fast as I could. An intense experience – to the smell of cold and cordite, and with the passing of shells overhead, the veiled women nodding and bowing, and the Madrid night we shared together – intense and not to be forgotten. When I'd finished, Captain Sam announced that a British volunteer had just given a violin recital. We both knew it wasn't that. The women on the floor gazed at me with benign indulgence, as though watching a neighbour's child just beginning to walk.

Around about dawn the shelling stopped and the restless children slept. But the families continued to sit round in clumps, forged like clinkers, black and immobile. I slipped out into the street, stepping over pieces of timber and piles of broken brick. In the building next door a great hole had appeared through which one could see the pale morning stars behind. A shell seemed to have passed right through one of the downstairs apartments and cleared out all the furniture except for the carpets. Nothing was left save for one mumbling old woman who sat stiffly upright in the middle of the room.

The stretcher-bearers arrived as I was passing. They took the woman's arm, but she snatched it away. Her thin grey legs stuck out in front of her, her mouth was twisted with shock. Her family had suddenly disappeared with the furniture, she said. She kept going through their names like a litany. 'Mi marido, Jacinta, Puelo, Ramon . . .' There must have been a dozen or more of them at least. They had been carried away as by some mighty wind, she said. She shook off her rescuers and would not move.

The streets around were blocked with debris. Carts and wagons were clearing up. Oddly enough, there had been no fire, only destruction. A few bodies lay under blankets along the pavements. Here and there somebody hobbled away. There were no shouts, no raised voices, just subdued, desultory, matter-of-fact exchanges as of neighbours starting another day.

The experience of being in Madrid again, contrasting its present cold desolation with the easy days of

my earlier visit, made me want to search out some
of the places I'd known.

I found the Puerta del Sol smothered in a pall of
greyness, and I remembered the one-time buzz of
the cafés, the tram bells, the cries of the lottery-
ticket sellers, the high-stepping servant girls with
their baskets of fresh-scrubbed vegetables, the parading young men and paunchy police at street
corners.

Now there was emptiness and silence – the cafés
closed, a few huddled women queuing at a shuttered
shop. Poor as it had been when I'd known it, there
had always been some sense of holiday in the town,
a defiant zest for small treats and pleasures, corner
stalls selling popcorn, carobs, sunflower seeds, vile
cigarettes, and little paper packets of bitter sweets.
Nothing now, of course, no smell of bread, oil, or
the reek of burnt fish that used to enliven the alleys
round the city centre – just a fusty aroma of horses,
straw, broken drains and fevered sickness.

I'd previously stayed at an old inn near the Calle
Echegarry, where I'd rented a room for sixpence a
night and had been looked after by Concha, a young
widow from Aranjuez. Carters from the sierras slept
with their beasts in the stables, and the landlord
kept a cow in the cellar.

I found the place transfigured. The great twenty-
foot doors, which for some five hundred years had

hung or swung on their elaborate tree-sized hinges, had now, after withstanding generations of war and plague, been torn down and burnt as fuel. The cobbled courtyard within, once crowded with mules and wagons, was now scattered with dismembered motor lorries. The slow carters, with their coatings of chaff and road dust, had been replaced by oil-faced repairmen and truck-drivers. In little over two years, this unchanged inn of Cervantes had become a repair depot for army vehicles. Indeed, in one corner, surrounded by an ardent group of greasy lads, they were even reassembling a captured Italian tank.

I went to seek out my old landlord and his wife, and found them freezing in the kitchen trying to heat some water over a smouldering brazier of oily rags. Coughing and weeping, they rose to embrace me, bidding the saints witness their surprise and delight. The thick smoky fumes made us grope for each other. There was much calling on the heavens in amazement. Eighteen months had transformed me, the young passing stranger of that summer, into a returned son, a reminder of tranquillity and the riches of peace. They gabbled eccentric endearments, and inquiries as to my health. Had I all my limbs sound? had I good boots? had I the gripe? did I want something to eat?

I insisted I wasn't hungry, but I let the landlord

take me to an underground tavern across the road, once a roaring kind of whorehouse, now shuttered and dark and used only by a few neighbours and soldiers. The innkeeper had changed much in the last two years, not an ageing of time but of things happening around him. This was not the towering man I'd known who used to throw the carters about and who once, when I was playing the violin in the courtyard, struck a chiming-clock with a brandy bottle for daring to interrupt. Thin now, and bent, shuffling and shaking, one of his magnificent dark eyes was half-closed and blind.

In the tavern he took me to join some of his friends, all old men dressed in black velvet suits.

'This is Lorenzo,' he said. 'Violinista, muy amigo. English or French – but it is not significant.' The old men showed no surprise, or much interest, in this information; but one of them poured me some wine, thin as the blood of a gnat.

A couple of militiamen came in and sat with their rifles across their knees. One was swearing and the other trying to quieten him. The old men watched them in silence, but sharpened their eyes.

The soldiers were Spanish, about my age, lean-faced and nervy.

'If I see another light in a window, I'll give it a blast with this,' said the younger one.

'But there were children there – you heard them.'

The young one leapt to his feet.

'Yes, and there were children killed last night.'

It had happened before, when night-shelling was heavy and precise – someone, some 'Franco agent', would have been flashing a torch from a rooftop or an upper window, and then, when the bombardment was heaviest, would toss a few grenades down into the street to confuse the fire-trucks and rescue parties.

After two winters of siege, the inside war was still active, and not everyone, even in this poor bare tavern, as he talked and moved his eyes about, could be absolutely sure of the man who sat beside him.

'We caught one of them, anyway,' the younger soldier said fiercely. 'Running across the tiles with a cart lamp.'

'Could have been trying to save his skin,' said someone.

'Did you arrest him?'

'Hell, no. We just threw him off the roof. He'd done enough. His body's outside in a barrow.'

Someone drew back the shutters on the cold grey street. A boy sat on the shafts of a hand-barrow, smoking. Stretched out on sacks between the high wooden wheels lay the crumpled body of a thin, old man. It was smartly dressed, and the head which hung down from the tailboard still wore a white-haired look of distinction.

'Know him?' asked a soldier.

'Yes,' someone said. 'You threw off the wrong one. That's Dr Cardenas. He has two sons in the Air Force . . .'

The two soldiers left; but there was no awkward silence, nor was the conversation changed too abruptly. First there was praise for the hero-pilots of the Republic – young eagles tackling the German vultures. Then in tones I was to remember – a mixture of death-bed reminiscence, shock, a reassurance of survival – the old men of Madrid drew together round their bare, bitter tables, and began to talk of the air war over the city; the black Junkers and Condors and snapping little German fighters, and the long night raids during the first winter of siege. 'There had never been such a sound before. The Devil's hand tearing holes in the sky. I was crossing the street. I saw a house come down before me. Like a man dropping a dusty cloak. Then there came a hot rushing wind which lifted me up and blew me into a fountain.' 'Soltero, down by the market. His house was cut in two. He woke to find half his bed and his wife had gone.' Then there were the fire-bombs, calculated, dropped on the old town and the poor. The Luftwaffe was clinical.

Franco had said that he was willing to wipe Madrid from the earth rather than let it remain 'in the hands of the Marxists'. So he gave it up to the

Luftwaffe, who were interested to see what mass-bombing could do to a major European city. Inhabitants in their thousands were splintered, broken, pulped or incinerated; survivors driven by fire from one district to another, forced to camp in the streets, in cellars, or the country. But the effect on the victims of that bombing – as it was often to prove in other cities later – was never the major cause of a people's defeat.

It was about midday now, and soon I would have to leave the tavern and report back to Captain Sam. Suddenly the street door broke open and a hunched shape crawled in, a huge cripple with withered legs. He'd opened the door with his head and now scampered around the room on all fours, with bits of motor tyre strapped to his hands and knees. I recalled him from earlier days – that fine, classical face, the powerful shoulders and thick arms of a boxer. 'Ay, Lorenzo!' he said with his deep-throated growl, as though he'd seen me but yesterday.

He'd always been a bit of a cynical wit and joker. Now, listening to the old men's tales of the air war, he added a few of his own – how his survival to date, for instance, depended on his God-given ability to scramble down drains quicker than anyone else. And did the honoured company of comrades re-member, he asked us, when that lone Fascist plane flew low over the city and released four little boxes attached to four separate parachutes? Wooden boxes, not bombs. Boxes tied with ribbon. People imagined they might be gifts. But when they were opened they were found to contain the carefully quartered body of a young Republican pilot. Ah, yes – very bad. But there'd been one flash of genuine kindness, added the cripple. When that other bomber flew over the city later one afternoon and dropped a fine, fat serrano ham. It was just before Christmas, and people hadn't seen ham for years. It fell on a man and tore off his arm.

I walked with the landlord back to his smoky kitchen, and we embraced, and his wife gave me some socks. Before leaving I slipped upstairs to see my old room, but found the door nailed up. As I came back down a voice called my name. Concha's rose cheeks had cooled, but her eyes were deeper than ever, though less assured than they had been. She had guided me the first time, now I was older, stronger. 'Man,' she said hesitantly, hanging back in the shadows. Then she put up a trembling hand and gently touched my mouth.

8

The Frozen Terraces of Teruel

Sam didn't return with us from Madrid. He stayed in the capital on other business. We found Tarazona half empty, the billets deserted, with most of the men gone to the Teruel front. The high heady news of Christmas victory had all changed since we'd been away. How had we not known what was happening? In Tarazona they knew well enough . . .

Franco had held Teruel for three years, a vulnerable line towards the coast, and when the Republicans recaptured it that Christmas it was thought that fortune had changed at last, that the days of retreat were over.

The worst was only beginning. The occupation of Teruel had been by Spanish troops only. No International Brigades were called on. Then Franco began his counter-attack with an artillery barrage so heavy, they said, that it clipped off the tops of the hills and completely altered the landscape. Protected by the Condor Legion, and two Generals in a twelve-carriage train, the Army Corps of Castile and

145

Galicia began to advance and the Republicans had to give up their brief-held prize.

As the weather worsened, the International Brigades were at last brought in. Fred Copeman, who commanded the British battalion, fell ill, and Bill Alexander took over. The 'Major Attlee' company received its christening, and thirteen men were killed the first day. Slowly the Republicans retreated outside the city, when the very war itself was halted by a four day blizzard, the worst in generations, during which men and their weapons froze together.

Such was the situation as we heard it when we got back from Madrid. A chill pall of wretchedness hung over the town. The chapel where I'd camped out formerly was being turned into a hospital, so I returned to the small house by the plaza, once quarters for black-coated Kassell and his crew, who it seemed had all departed. Instead, it was now occupied by two mysterious brothers from Cartagena, stern ascetics who scarcely spoke. They'd stripped the villa of its decorations, its posters and maps, and left only bare walls across which they'd painted VITORIA! in large red letters.

It was said that they were ex-priests, and they certainly seemed single-minded enough, and had a zealous, passionate hatred for General Franco and his words – and were not all that fond of us either.

They were men of authority, a new power in Tarazona, and I felt that their taking over of this minor headquarters – so long dominated by Kassell, Political Commissars, British Company Commanders, and instructors – may well have marked, in its small way, the beginning of the break-up of the International Brigades. For these men were not internationalists or politicos, but simply Spanish patriots. They seemed to wish this to be understood.

The brothers – both young, perhaps in their early thirties – had sharp, blue-tempered chins, and the eyes of religious assassins. They were self-mortifiers, too, and slept on the floor without covering, and sometimes walked barefoot in the snow.

One morning, soon after my return, they called me into their back room, together with a Portuguese youth named Serrano, and said they were sending us up to Teruel. I remember the interview in the 'office' – the brothers wearing single blankets like hairshirts, both squatting on the floor, but making us stand. They looked at handsome young Serrano with lechery and contempt; they looked at me as possible fuel for a burning.

'Portuguese and Inglese,' one said to the other. 'Worse than French. No salt in the bone.'

We left the next morning at dawn. Our orders were few and ambiguous. I gathered the brothers wanted us out of the place. We drove out of Tarazona in brutal weather in a lorry rattling with thick chained wheels. The squat olive trees on the hillside rolled in the cutting wind like bundles of black barbed wire. Serrano had a heavy cold now and was no longer pretty; he was also intensely miserable. We had rations for one day, but the journey was likely to take two. We huddled together against a roll of tarpaulins.

We were the only passengers in the truck; the rest, it seemed, was cargo. I'd been told we were carrying ammunition, but we were bouncing too light for that. Under the tarpaulins there was only donkey harness, the gaily tasselled stuff they wore down in Andalucia. Why were we carrying such rubbish to the front, I wondered?

About noon we reached the hills, but the snow was heavy, so we pulled up under a bridge. Our driver climbed out of his cab and stumbled round to join us, followed by a small and muffled figure. In a cloud of breath they climbed into the back of the truck, and the driver asked for a cigarette. From the snow's bright glare one saw a flushed, drunkard's face, darkly sprouting with bristles, a powerful torso, and small bent legs. All that was visible of his crouching companion was a pair of deep slanting eyes peering through a thick wrapping of scarves.

The driver spoke rough bullying Spanish with a Russian accent – the first I had heard for weeks. His small companion crawled towards him and answered with the low voice of a girl, agreeing, placating, wheedling. He dug into his pocket, produced a tin of sardines, and slowly broke it open. Then he scooped out one of the brittle little fish, gave it a shake, and held it in front of the girl. She lifted the scarf from her face, opened her mouth like a bird's, and he popped the oily morsel between her lips. She seemed to swallow it whole, with only the faintest flicker of her throat, then stretched her mouth open for more. So he patiently fed her till the tin was empty, wiping her lips at last with his sleeve.

He'd found her in the mountains, he said; thin and bony as a stork's nest. He was fattening her up to be a proper armful. All she does, he said, is eat and sleep. And when she slept, he ate.

There was something Grand Guignol about these two, their incongruity and their different sizes, he bull-like, a great black minotaur, and she – in spite of her wrapping of scarves – no more than a doll. With her face uncovered she was waxenly beautiful and not more than fourteen, I would have thought. Was he the father-protector he appeared to be, or she as childish as she seemed?

Serrano, who suddenly came awake in a paroxysm of coughing, rolled off the tarpaulin and asked where we were. I explained about the snow, the bridge, the Russian driver and the girl, but he only shook his head and moaned. The driver opened another tin of sardines and shared it with us, pushing back the girl into a corner as he did so. He seemed to be loaded with food, he even had bread, and the pockets of his greatcoat clinked and clattered. Serrano asked him why we were carrying donkey harness instead of guns, and the man laughed and said did we want to be blown up?

The girl gazed long and silently at Serrano, and was about to say something, when the Russian took her back to his cab, pulled the truck on to the road and began the long slow climb up the sierra. The snow had thinned a bit now, and came only in large flaky gusts as though someone was opening and shutting a gigantic door. Along the roadside, among the rocks and tree stumps, we passed strings of broken-down trucks and wagons. Men, swaddled in blankets, crouched in the cabins or huddled by blowing fires. There seemed to be no traffic at all going towards the front, it all appeared to be coming away towards us – lorries, strings of mules; occasionally a scattered bunch of men, and now and then an ancient high-roofed ambulance.

We drove in silence, in a dumb state of nothing, having no part of what we saw, nor any certain direction. Serrano let his head fall lower and lower between his shoulders, and his shoulders between his knees. Even the shouting Russian in the front had suddenly grown silent. Then as darkness fell, and the snow squalls lessened, quick flashes of fire, like summer lightning, began to dapple along the hill ridges ahead of us.

The road was bad now, cluttered with rocks and holes and the litter of smashed-up vehicles. We stopped by a derelict barn, sheltered in a kind of quarry, and bedded down there for the night. The Russian propped his girl in the corner, helped us build a fire, then handed round more sardines. He was now the big shaggy leader, the guardian, the provider, and we began to wonder what we would have done without him. Shuffling round on his knees, smacking our hands with bread, then hobbling away to feed the girl, his busy bulk seemed to crowd the barn like some amiable restless bear.

With the fire and the food Serrano was on the mend, his fine curls glistened, as did his eyes. And the girl watched him silently, first uncovering her face, then more slyly her shoulders, wriggling inch by inch towards him. In spite of the cold, her expression was one of simple rapture, which I don't think the boy even noticed. But the driver did: he cuffed her ears with his paws and pushed her back whimpering against the wall. Then he came and squatted by the fire and told us the story of his life, which, being Russian, was long and dank.

At intervals, in the distance, we heard the snapping of gunfire, sound sharpened by the edge of frost. So Teruel was not far, and the front still awake, but we were too exhausted to care. To the epic drone of the driver's story Serrano and I fell asleep. The sleep was unhealthy and broken. The gunfire drew nearer. I woke to the blank glimmer of a dying fire. Serrano lay curled and twitching like a dreaming dog, his mouth giving faint little yelps; while sprawled on his back in the corner, the Russian snored heavily, the girl held over his chest like a blanket.

It was one of the coldest nights I could remember. I lay with my hands between my thighs, my clenched teeth chattering, my overcoat crackling with frost. A deadening numbness assailed the toes and fingertips, and the nostrils stung as though split by skewers. Eventually, I got to my feet and stamped about. Snow whipped in gusts through holes in the roof. Indifferent, in his corner, the Russian continued to snore, while the girl on his belly sniffled and wept.

Just before daylight the gunfire stopped, and I woke Serrano − who seemed to be sleeping in a posture too close to death, his mouth hanging open like a poisoned rodent's. I lit a new fire and boiled some snow and we dipped our last crusts of bread in it. Suddenly, as the fire blazed up, we saw that the Russian's corner was empty. Then we heard from outside the mad whirring of a starting handle, a shout, an engine bursting into life and then fade as the truck drove away.

We had been dumped. The driver hadn't even said goodbye, or even left us a single tin of sardines. We were on our own – wherever that might be – without direction, orders or food. What was I doing in these Spanish mountains, anonymous of purpose, with this pretty Portuguese boy of whom I knew nothing?

As the late daylight came, I left Serrano huddled by the fire, and went outside and got my first view of Teruel. It stood some five miles distant and slightly above us, a gleaming city of ice, its cathedral, castle, turrets, towers, all dusted with a silver, shimmering light. A city of silence, without dimension; it could have been a life-size mural, or an intimately carved ivory for some medieval Cardinal or Pope. A perfect relic, in its brilliant stillness, chaste and bloodless as a martyr's tomb. Yet already, I was to learn, within the last few days, its citizens were walling up and massacring each other.

Its silence, now, could have been the silence of exhaustion after the excesses and bombardments of the night. Its sleep, not the sleep of peace and restoration, but a readying of strength for further outrage. So in this brief moment of armistice Teruel hushed itself, bathed in the mother-of-pearl morning, motionless, save for the tendrils of slender smoke spiralling into the sky.

Presently, as I stood there, my back to the barn, blowing on my fingers and watching the town, I saw three figures approaching in the distance, running doubled up, in little stumbling spurts. They were roly-poly bundles, dressed in fluttering blankets, and they fanned out to encircle the place. As they drew nearer, popping up and down like hares or pheasants, I wondered if they thought they were invisible. I slipped back into the barn and woke up Serrano, and we watched through a hole in the wall. The smoke from our fire must have drawn their attention, but they seemed in no hurry to come to close quarters. Then I heard one call to the others to keep their heads well down, that he'd soon 'flush out the little buggers'. His lilting voice had a South Welsh accent, and he lifted a grenade to his teeth.

I leapt out of the barn, held up my empty hands, and shouted to him not to bother. 'Come on over,' I said. 'We're from Tarazona.' After a silence, they all straightened up and joined us. The Welshman came first, dragging a giant foot wrapped in a bundle of sacking. 'Sod the bugger,' he said, prodding the lump with his musket. 'Well, what's going on here, then, boyo?'

The three stood round me, awkward, dumpy, ageless in their woollen mufflers. Well might they ask, I thought; I didn't know. I took them inside to the last of the fire. They crouched around on their haunches, shuddering with cold, gasping and blowing on the ashes. In their damp balaclavas only their eyes were visible and these darted about like mice in a basket.

'Who's that?' asked the Welshman, jerking his head towards Serrano, who was rocking on his heels and blubbering and sneezing. I tried to explain who he was, and realized I didn't know either.

The Welshman guessed it, then turned to Serrano and addressed him in perfect Spanish. He got no answer but sighs and moans. 'It 'ould pay us to get rid of 'im I reckon.'

His companions got to their feet and began to turn the boy over with their rifles. Serrano went limp like a doll. The Welshman spat.

'Bin on patrol all night,' he growled, 'just to pick up two tarts from Tarazona. Well, no offence, you – but just look at *him*.'

Fear had curled Serrano's hair with a glorious shine. His fragile fingers clasped one of the soldier's boots.

'Might as well,' said the soldier, cocking his rifle. He had a teasing Liverpool accent.

At that moment, with a clapping of giant hands, the bombardment began again.

156

'Well, come on boys,' said the Welshman, almost cheerful now, 'better get you all back to base.'

Then we were out of the barn and running, bent low, following the limping, shouting Welshman. The bombardment was not so distant as it had been, the ground shook as though being beaten, the air screamed and tore, and we all fell flat, face down.

Under bombardment, the body takes over the mind; it stiffens and melts, the mouth floods and dries, and all one's senses rush to the back of one's neck. The barn disappeared in a woosh of clay and splinters, and I tried to bury myself among the slush-covered rocks.

When a shell hit the ground and exploded near by, the snow rose in the air like a dirty ghost, and hung there spikily billowing, before collapsing into the ground again. Such apparitions increased all around me, lifting, hovering and falling, together with the brutal rending and peeling back of the air, and the knowledge that under bombardment one has no courage.

I learned only later that this great build-up of shelling marked the end of the Teruel battle. Franco's troops, helped by Italian tanks and planes, were hitting back at the fortress city. The Republican forces, together with the International Brigades, began their inevitable withdrawal, clinging briefly to the open heights and little gullies

157

round the walls, before continuing their retreat southwards and towards the sea. The gift of Teruel at Christmas had become for the Republicans no more than a poisoned toy. It was meant to be the victory that would change the war; it was indeed the seal of defeat.

Pinned down throughout much of the morning, with the Welshman's great foot in view, about noon I heard him call out, 'Come on, then, follow me!' and saw his foot bouncing before me like a snow-ball.

The landscape around showed all the rubbish of failure, the end of charity and hope. The fate of new Spain – that 'arid square' – was decided among the frozen terraces of Teruel. As the gully widened, the Welshman leading, we clambered among more trucks and debris. Three soldiers lay propped against a wall, their bodies half-stripped by the wind, their flesh a bluish-black. Their eyes were open, glazed like ice. Most certainly they had frozen to death.

I don't think the Welshman knew where he eventually brought us – a bunker scraped out of rock and snow and half-covered by a sheet of tin. There was a dog, and a cooking-pot, and a few shivering men eating out of rusty cans. Grey-faced and in rags, their heads moved in quick animal jerks as they ate, up and down, left and right, as though hunted. They were Spanish and the Welshman hurried past them without speaking and scrambled further off down the hill with Serrano.

The Spaniards asked who I was. Ingles, I said. Then why had I come all this way too late? They were the Spanish Army. They didn't need the help of foreigners. Or they needed the help of the world.

But they let me stay with them. 'All your comrades have gone anyway.' They gave me an old Winchester rifle with a couple of clips of cartridges. 'At least you can shoot yourself.'

I stayed with the Spaniards for several days in the frozen vault of their bunker. Never had I seen any men so drained of hope and spirit. Except when the bucket of food came up each morning they seldom stirred from the foetal position in which they hunched themselves. They had no field-telephone, the place seemed to have no purpose; and their leader – an ex-schoolmaster from Talavera – said he had no idea what his men were supposed to be doing.

'Papa Guido' they called him, their voices intoning with bitterness. His eyes were plum-coloured with fear and exhaustion, and somewhere about his person he kept a tasselled cap which every so often he clapped on his head, whereupon everybody saluted him gravely. Stowed away in their almost speechless lethargy a black humour sometimes showed itself.

They'd had ten days' bombardment, said Guido, and been overrun twice, though no one seemed to notice them hidden away under the bunker. But one of them had been bayoneted by chance by a running Moor who had returned to finish him off. The wounded man, middle-aged, rather plump, swung half between coma and delirium. Sometimes he sang in a faint, faraway voice, or lay inert, covered by dead men's coats. His bleeding had stopped, but there seemed not much hope. They'd been trying to get him away, but no help came.

There was a lull, then one night a ghostly fog curled around us, a heavy vapour half-drawn from our breath and half from the circling banks of snow. It brought with it a deadlier cold than ever. With this, Guido seemed to come awake from his torpor. Stuttering madly, he began formally to address his troops, issue commands, and divide the night into watches.

Away to the left of the city we saw lights moving about and heard clear but distant shouts. 'They're coming back,' said Guido, touching his lower lip with his finger in an effort to still his stutter. And sure enough, in the morning, they came.

A long burst of shellfire straddled over us just before daylight, followed by the rattling metal of tanks and their sharp coughing guns, and the swooping buzz of Italian aircraft above. The main attack

160

of the armour was up ahead of us, even so we were briefly overrun; our machine-gun blew up, and we pulled back down the gully, scrambling and falling over the ice. First, I remember a running close-up of the enemy – small, panting little men, red-faced boys, frantically spitting Moors. There was the sudden bungled confrontation, the breathless hand-to-hand, the awkward pushing, jabbing, grunting, swearing, death a moment's weakness or slip of the foot away. Then we broke and raced off, each man going alone, each the gasping centre of his own survival.

I headed for the old barn where I'd spent my first night. I lay in a state of sick paralysis. I had killed a man, and remembered his shocked, angry eyes. There was nothing I could say to him now. Tanks rattled by and cries receded. I began to have hallucinations and breaks in the brain. I lay there knowing neither time nor place. Some of our men found me, I don't know who they were, and they drove me back speechless to Tarazona.

Was this then what I'd come for, and all my journey had meant – to smudge out the life of an unknown young man in a blur of panic which in no way could affect victory or defeat?

9

Way Back

The white daylight was like pain; I could see it and feel it – a plastic stretch of silence pulled over the face. I sat on the chapel steps; half-blind, half-drugged, while melting ice trickled over my feet. The sound of war, several days old and imprinted in the back of my head, seemed ready to return at the touch of a button. The man sitting beside me wore a crumpled white coat. He looked like a doctor or butcher.

'Comrade, we're sending you back to London,' he said.

A tubby young man, with a French moustache: the Political Commissar of Tarazona.

I said I didn't want to go.

'You'd be more use to us there. After all, you're not much use to us here. You could write about us, make speeches, paint posters – or something . . .' He gave me his soft butcher's smile, patted me on the arm, stood up and left, taking his white coat with him.

There was no one to say goodbye to in Tarazona;

they were all of them gone, dead, deserted, or swept away in the snows. I collected my blanket, and canvas bag, and took a truck down to Albacete. The soldiers there, mostly Spanish now, flapped about in their mud-edged ponchos. There was a moist scummy air of impending spring, but a spring without warmth or profit.

I dropped my bags at the barracks and went round to the tavern where previously we'd sucked sugar and drunk crushed acorns. There were no acorns now, and the victory posters were peeling from the walls like skin. War-cries and slogans, reversed, in-growing, perversely coiled on themselves.

The young Spanish soldiers, squatting around, were not as conventionally foul-mouthed as usual; instead their speech now was almost clerical and precise, using abstract and ritual phrases.

'We were outnumbered. We were betrayed. We were punished. God froze us.'

'God what?'

'He froze us with his mighty breath.'

The talk was still of Teruel; the unforgivable, unimaginable, the snatching away of the cup; the sudden tilt from light into darkness.

I left the tavern and found two men under a bridge, one bandaging the other's knee. The first was about my age, his chin a tar-brush of beard; the other was younger, and beardless.

'My brother,' nodded the youth, gently twisting the bandage.

'He followed me . . . I couldn't get rid of him,' said the younger boy.

'I didn't. I went with the major.'

'How did you find me then?'

'I smelt you out like a rat.'

'Rather some fat-breasted nun had found me!'

His muddy trousers had been split up the seam and a wound ran from knee to groin. His brother had lightly bandaged half of it, and now cleaned the knee with water from a can. The edge of the broken flesh was green and the man was sweating gently.

'No decent nurse would come near you, porco,' said the youth, propping him into a sitting position. 'I got you here, and I'll get you home. So try not to be a burden.'

He rolled him slowly, carefully, on to a little hand-cart standing by, and pushed him off through the melting snow.

It was not going to be easy getting me back to England. I'd entered illegally and must return the same way. But the general opinion was: go I must. I reported to Captain Sam, the intelligence officer, in his little office off the main street. But something had happened to him since last we met; he seemed drowsier, plumper, more evasive. He sat in his

German flying-jacket, not quite looking at me, picking at a saucer of olives. I wondered what the winter had done to change that spry little killer into this heavy somnambulist lump.

'All you got to do,' he said, 'is get to Barcelona, then over the border – then it's up to you.'

He seemed amused by this, and opened a drawer.

'They told me to give you this.'

He handed me an envelope which contained my passport and five swoony Chanel-scented pound notes. Still in their envelope inscribed Socorro Rojo in the girl's galloping cumulus handwriting. I could have wished the pound notes less pungent and the girl's letter unresurrected, but I stuffed the lot in my shirt.

'You know, Lorenzo,' said Sam, looking out of the window, 'I've often wondered about you. Just what your game is. What you've been doing here. They say you don't know which side to get on a bus.'

He tore a form from a book, and stamped and signed it. Then he handed it to me gravely.

'Your Safe Conduct,' he said. 'It won't be much use to you, though. As you're not officially here.'

The railway to Barcelona had just been bombed again, so I joined a convoy of trucks. We did the trip in one night, staying close together and keeping an eye on one another's rear-lamps. It was a long cold night, sitting on sacks of sodden straw and sliding about at each curve in the road. The passengers were mostly army (or ex-army, as I was). There was also a middle-aged politico clutching a crocodile brief-case who huddled in a corner and kept up a whispered commentary of bitter reproaches addressed to Azaña Largo Caballero. As for me, all I wished was an end to this somehow; a quick sharp bomb, or a lucky escape across Europe, and to get back to her bed and rest.

We drove fast and bumpily through the night, tailboards and mudguards clattering, racing for the most part without lights over the stony plateau, the frightened politico whispering and whining, the driver shouting, the reek of burnt petrol rising from the floor. Stopping under a blue shaded light of a sleeping village, or to the muffled torches of sentries, or for freezing wine in a bar. Then the pleas of women and girls wanting to be taken to the city, the good-natured obscenities of the driver, families sitting round wood fires under the broken arches of stables, running over to beg for lifts to other villages; sounds of doom, hysteria, shrieks of laughter, cries – everybody wishing to be somewhere else.

We drove for about twelve hours that night, refuelling at road-blocks, and reached the outskirts of Barcelona in a late grey dawn. After the medieval towns and villages of central Spain, Barcelona revealed an alien industrial Europe, long squat suburbs and shabby concrete factories – a language far more cynical, knowing and enervating than the primitive naïveties of Castile.

The small greedy streets crossed each other like lines in a ledger, leading finally to the grand ruled boulevards. Compared with dandy, spendthrift Madrid, Barcelona had been the clever, rich uncle, aloof, scarcely Spanish at all. All its fine calculations, now, seemed blurred, blotted and cancelled. Across banks and offices sagged the war's first banner of defiance and challenge, muted and fading as the grey figures in the streets.

Jaime, the man I had been told to seek out, lived at the top of an old Victorian-style house down a narrow side-street at the harbour end of Las Ramblas. The house bulged with men and meaty women and thumped with squeals and laughter. Girls' faces like pom-poms peeped from half-open doorways. There were such aromas of oils and powders and warm flesh on the stairs that winter and war seemed wiped away.

Jaime, a tough young Catalan with a Prussian moustache, welcomed me into his tiny attic. Packed on shelves round the walls he had books and records and pretty Tanagra figures. There was a wind-up gramophone with a horn in a corner on which he was playing a Beethoven sonata. He turned it off as I entered, and the happy din from downstairs surged up through gaps in the stairs.

I'd met Jaime in Tarazona. Besides Catalan, he spoke Spanish, Basque, French, German, and English with a Dublin accent. He was a Professor of Theology from the University of Seville, and was also a wounded veteran from the Ebro front.

He showed me his new wooden leg, beautifully turned and finished, and knocked up by a local guitar-maker.

'Rosewood, cedar and ebony,' he said, and stamped on the floor. 'When they play music, he dances.'

He gave me some brandy, and told me what I had to do. It was like taking part in some surrealist chess, where pawns became Kings and Queens without warning, and the value of the pieces changed in mid-play. The Police, the Army, the City Militia, the Syndicates, all had power, but its order they said altered daily.

'Anyway, it will be no trouble, I promise you. Present yourself to the Secretariat. They'll give you an exit visa. Say nothing – it will be all right.'

He must have seen the look of doubt on my face.

'It happens all the time. Don't worry. They know what we're up to. But if you fall among fools – destroy your papers.'

Jaime, grinning thinly, was giving the impression of the big spider with his fingers on all the webs, controlling the city's sprawling underbrush and all its secret comings and goings.

Well, I believed him, and strolled up Las Ramblas and presented myself straight away at Police Headquarters, where, in some grand inner office, they examined my passport and Chanel-scented pound notes, and promptly arrested me as deserter and spy.

I asked at least could I have my scented money back, but the notes were shovelled into a drawer. The Chief gave me a straight, hard look. 'That goes towards the "Effort",' he said. 'After all, you didn't do much for it, did you?'

So once more I was being marched along the streets between two steel-helmeted soldiers armed with fixed bayonets. To the afternoon crowd I was a figure of just casual interest, children and girls gave me only the briefest of glances. A young man under guard, especially a blond young foreigner, was clearly no longer a remarkable spectacle in the city. Though one whiskered old man hobbled out of a doorway, crossed the road, and pinched my thighs.

'Don't shoot him,' he said. 'Just give him to me. I'll take him home to the wife.'

The guards marched me on into a large black building near the docks and pushed me through a side-door, saying, 'We've brought you another one.' My reception was disinterested, no names in a book, no questions; I was merely told to wait. The vast ante-room was like a Dickensian debtors' prison; a dark, shadowy space only dimly lit, and crowded with men, women and children sitting around on the floor. Some cooked, or played games, or slept or fumbled. There was a high chattering and glitter of teeth. I saw men in old tattered uniforms, with bandaged legs, surrounded by what seemed to be mothers, wives and cousins. They stroked the men's feet and fed them soup. The place was a chamber of limbo.

After an hour or so, I was taken to an iron grille which spanned the far end of the room. Behind were the cells of the prison proper, and there they installed me without word or ceremony. Each cell had a couple of bunks and a cracked hole in the floor, down which a trickle of water flowed. In my cell I washed away every piece of paper that could identify me – notes, army cards, pencilled instructions, the Salvo Conductos, even the girl's wanton and bubbling letters. Then anonymous, unknown and I hoped forgotten, I settled in my cell with a companion who never spoke. I hoped it would stay like that. I wanted no sudden keys in the lock, or

my name called in the night. I hoped that by now
I'd just be a blank in the system.

I stayed in that cell for about three weeks. No
guard or authority came near me. There was a heavy
damp staleness about the air as though the walls
were hung with sour blankets. After a few days I
began to understand what it meant to rot in gaol.
Daylight moved slowly across a distant skylight.
No food or drink was provided. We sipped water
from the metal cup chained near the spout in the
corner, and each day, about noon, a nun would
bring us a small flat sandwich and pass it through
the bars in silence.

In twenty-four hours it was all we got, and how
we longed for noon. But that sandwich, even
whiter, smaller than the nun's quiet hand, flavoured
on the inside by a thin scraping of mincemeat and
on the outside by her ineffable fragrance of touch,
what a feast it was to our shackled appetites and
hungers. And how voluptuously remembered since.

Meanwhile, apart from these wisplike visits, we
were left alone. Nobody came and nothing
happened. There were no shouting inspections or
calling out for exercise or punishment. We seemed
to have been abandoned. This was hard to believe
in a huge military jail like this, but to begin with I
was glad of it.

Then after the second week, lying in the twilit

vacancy of my cell, I gradually grew concerned by the silence. My companion had disappeared. What fate, I wondered, were they storing up for me? And when would they come to declare it? After the third week I began scheming to smuggle out messages for help, to Jaime, or anyone at all. Three weeks, without threat or sentence or even occasional persecution seemed thoughtless indeed.

I was sick now, shivering on the concrete floor, scraping the mould from the walls with my finger-nails. An escalating series of panics broke away from each other and led nowhere except back to my head. Only night, the black skylight, and the noon-whispering nun bearing the half sandwich in her small lace-lined basket, looped the empty silence of the sprawling jail.

Deliverance came, suddenly, unexpectedly, and with a casual lack of drama. A shabby old porter was unlocking my door, and I saw that he had no gun. 'Go away,' he said, 'out!'; and he gave me a daft grandfatherly smile that was a thin red slit in his face. 'What a surprise,' he said, 'eh?' And he thumped me in the ribs, then fumblingly unlocked the outer grille. We walked through a network of passages to the ground floor, through half-light and darkness, through whispers of sound and the smell of unwashed men drawing their body heat from one another.

Back again in the huge open hall of the gaol, still crowded with women and barefoot children, I picked my way through the waiting, watchful, ragged groups, and followed where the old trusty led me.

'There's your friend,' he said at last, nodding towards the door. It was a surprise indeed.

Leaning against a pillar near the entrance was a short tubby man wearing a smart overcoat and trilby hat. He gave me a shy warm smile, slightly tinged with embarrassment. It was Bill Rust, editor of the *Daily Worker*.

'You should be in London,' he said. 'How d'you manage to end up here?'

I told him I'd been following instructions.

'Ah, Jaime – yes.' He shifted uncomfortably. 'Well, come on. I've got a car outside.'

And so he had, with all my bags piled in the back of it. I was free, sprung suddenly from my mildewed cell into the clear air of the Barcelona night. Rust had been having a drink that evening with the Chief of Police, who mentioned he'd an unexplained Englishman down in the jail. Rust guessed it was me. Vouch for him, you can have him, said the Chief.

I was glad, but a bit sore at the mess I'd been in.

'So you came as soon as you heard?' I said.

'You were lucky. I don't drink with police every night.'

'But I've been stuck down here for over three weeks.'

'You could have been stuck here for the rest of your life.'

Rust drove me to his flat, high up in one of the boulevards, and said I should stay there till things got untangled. He lit a geyser for a bath, gave me a tumblerful of whisky, then cooked me a piled plateful of corned-beef hash. He was a quiet, gentle man, tough with bureaucrat bullies, but a kindly uncle to such strays as myself. I stayed in his flat for two or three days, not over-eager to return to the streets in case I got picked up again. To keep me occupied he asked me to sort out his filing cards, which were in shoe-boxes and needed putting in alphabetical order. Cards with the names and addresses of British and Irish volunteers; next of kin (if any); dates of enlistment; Brigade postings; brief histories, comments. There must have been five or six hundred of them. Many – more than half – were marked 'killed in action' or 'missing', at such fronts as Brunete, Guadalajara, the Ebro. Public schoolboys, undergraduates, men from coal mines and mills, they were the ill-armed advance scouts in the, as yet, unsanctified Second World War. Here were the names of dead heroes, piled into little cardboard boxes, never to be inscribed later in official Halls of Remembrance. Without recognition, often ridiculed, they saw what was coming, jumped the gun, and went into battle too soon.

Rust was in and out of the flat most of the day, and in the evening we drank whisky and talked. He never spoke of his newspaper, or the war or his connection with it, but told mild stories of childhood atrocities. He asked me no questions, except about my health, which seemed to concern him closely. There was, indeed, something almost nannyish about his care of me, even to the extent of giving me his card-index to play with.

On the third day, taking no chances, Rust drove me round to the French Consulate and the city Police Headquarters, and got me my exit visas. The officer, who had already swiped my Chanel-scented pound notes, crisply stamped my passport: salé sin dinero – departed without money. 'Farewell, brother,' he said. 'I think you've not been defrauded.'

Jaime came to the station to give me last-minute instructions, together with coded addresses in Paris and London. Also apologies and excuses which didn't matter now and were unearned anyway. Already in my mind I'd left this doomed city and country, where women queued hopelessly outside shops, hospitals and prisons, waiting in the rain for miracles.

The night train to the frontier was waiting – crowded, murmuring, without lights, unheated, and smelling of unwashed wounds. I found a space in a tiny wood-slatted compartment already dotted with the red stubs of cigarettes. At first we stumbled slowly through the shiny black suburbs of the city while searchlights moved over the sea. Nothing could be heard but half-stifled coughing, heavy breathing, and the faint, frightened moan of a woman. Reaching the open country we picked up speed, in a steady slouching way, and my companions suddenly found their voices with a carefree release of bravado. Two of them were obviously from the same village up the coast. They were reunited and returning home.

'You remember Don Anselmo – the fish-factor?'

'Of course I remember him.'

'A thief and a robber he was.'

'A peseta a day he paid us – before they shot him.'

'Who shot him?'

'Well, the Committee shot him, wasn't it?'

'Yes, the Committee, they shot him. They shot a lot of them.'

'A little peseta a day – God shame him.'

It was a shaking out of justice, hoarse agreement all round, then with prolonged coughing and shuffling everybody settled to sleep. Cigarettes went out, and there was silence, except for the distant moan of the woman.

We arrived at Port Bou in the dirty light of dawn. On the platform stood a bunch of grey-faced men. Their hands were manacled and they were dressed in rags of uniform and guarded by a couple of old veterans with muskets. Deserters, someone said, trying to scramble out over the mountains. When I came in, I remembered, coming the other way, something like this had also happened to me.

Now I was on my way back, with official papers to help me, salé sin dinero, and little else. The two mountain boulders I'd walked between, on my way into Spain, had seemed almost too simple a way to enter a war. In reverse, it was even simpler; our train took a gulping breath, left the underworld behind it, and screwed through the short tunnel between Port Bou and Cerebere. Curtains were lifted, we saw fresh morning skies, neon-lit cafés, and smelt the hot fat butter of France . . .

At dawn the next day I arrived at Victoria station and saw the cloud of her breath where she waited. She looked at my hands, then my face, and gave her short jackal laugh. I sniffed the cold misty fur of her hair.

As we drove north she watched me as much as she watched the road. 'Well, I hope you're pleased with yourself,' she said. 'Didn't give me a thought, did you? I've been through absolute hell – you know that? I even went to a call-box one night, a public phone-box – can you imagine? – and I got right through to Socorro Rojo, Albacete. Just think – across France, and those frontiers – and all Spain and that war . . . It took me three hours, and I was crying all the time. I just wanted to talk to you, *talk* to you, can you understand? A man was watching me from a car, and kept giving me money for the phone. No wonder you look so smug.'

Then I was back in her flat. In high wealthy Hampstead. She drew me in with her blue steady gaze. I remember the flowers on the piano, the white sheets on her bed, her deep mouth, and love without honour.